CHILTE
WALKS

HERTFORDSHIRE, BEDFORDSHIRE
& NORTH BUCKINGHAMSHIRE

Nick Moon

This book is one of a series of three which provide a comprehensive coverage of walks throughout the whole of the Chiltern area (as defined by the Chiltern Society). The walks included vary in length from 2.1 to 11.1 miles, but are mainly in the 5- to 7-mile range popular for half-day walks, although suggestions of possible combinations of walks are given for those preferring a full day's walk.

Each walk gives details of nearby places of interest and is accompanied by a specially drawn map of the route which also indicates local pubs and a skeleton road network.

The author, Nick Moon, has lived in or regularly visited the Chilterns all his life and has, for over 25 years, been an active member of the Chiltern Society's Rights of Way Group, which seeks to protect and improve the area's footpath and bridleway network. Thanks to the help and encouragement of the late Don Gresswell MBE, he was introduced to the writing of books of walks and has since written or contributed to a number of publications in this field.

OTHER PUBLICATIONS BY NICK MOON

Chiltern Walks Trilogy

Chiltern Walks 1 :	Hertfordshire, Bedfordshire and North Buckinghamshire : Book Castle new edition 2001
Chiltern Walks 2 :	Buckinghamshire : Book Castle new edition 1997
Chiltern Walks 3 :	Oxfordshire and West Buckinghamshire : Book Castle new edition 2001

Oxfordshire Walks

Oxfordshire Walks 1 :	Oxford, the Cotswolds and the Cherwell Valley : new edition 1998
Oxfordshire Walks 2 :	Oxford, the Downs and the Thames Valley : new edition 2001

Family Walks
Family Walks 1 : Chilterns – South : 1997
Family Walks 2 : Chilterns – North : 1998

The D'Arcy Dalton Way across the Oxfordshire Cotswolds and Thames Valley, 1999

The Chiltern Way : 2000

First published April 1993
New edition July 1996
New edition May 2001
by The Book Castle
12 Church Street, Dunstable, Bedfordshire

© Nick Moon, 2001

Computer Typeset by J. L. Miller (Keyword), Aldbury, Herts
Printed in Great Britain by Antony Rowe Ltd., Chippenham, Wilts.

ISBN 1 903747 00 7

Contents

POSSIBLE LONGER WALKS PRODUCED BY COMBINING WALKS DESCRIBED IN THE BOOK

Walks	Miles	Km	Walks	Miles	Km
2A + 3	13.2	21.2	14A + 15	16.9	27.2
2A + 3 + 4A	19.6	31.5	14C + 15	13.1	21.0
2A + 4A	13.3	21.4	17 + 18A	13.1	21.1
2A + 4A + 5	20.8	33.4	19 + 20	14.4	23.1
2B + 3	12.1	19.4	21A + 22	15.0	24.1
2B + 3 + 4B	17.9	28.8	23 + 24	13.4	21.5
2B + 4B	11.6	18.7	23 + 24 + 25	21.6	34.8
2B + 4B + 5	19.1	30.7	23 + 24 + 26A	21.7	34.9
4A + 5	13.9	22.3	23 + 24 + 26B	15.3	24.7
4B + 5	13.3	21.4	23 + 25	15.1	24.3
7A + 8	16.7	26.9	23 + 25 + 26A	20.3 or 23.7	32.7 or 38.1
7A + 14A	16.9	27.2	23 + 25 + 26B	17.3	27.9
7A + 14B	14.3	23.0	24 + 25 + 26B	17.5	28.2
7B+ 8	11.0	17.6	25 + 26A	13.1 or 16.4	21.1 or 26.5
7C + 14A	14.2	22.8	25 + 26B	10.1	16.3
7C + 14B	11.6	18.6	26A + 27	15.7	25.2
9 + 12A	13.6	22.0	26A + 28	16.9	27.3
9 + 12A + 13	21.5	34.5	26C + 27	13.7	22.1
9 + 12B	12.7	20.5	26C + 27 + 28	21.8	35.1
9 + 12B + 13	20.6	33.1	26C + 28	15.0	24.1
9 + 13	14.8	23.8	27 + 28	14.6	23.5
13 + 17	12.6	20.2	27 + 28 + 29	21.8	35.2
13 + 17 + 18A	19.3	31.1	28 + 29	14.6	23.6

Cover Photograph: View from Highpark Wood looking across Water End towards Gaddesden Place. (Walk 7). © Nick Moon.

Introduction

This book of walks is one of three covering the whole of the Chilterns from the Goring Gap on the River Thames to the Hitchin Gap in North Hertfordshire. The area covered by this volume includes the whole of the Hertfordshire and Bedfordshire Chilterns as well as the detached part of the Buckinghamshire Chilterns north of Tring. From a geographical point of view the county boundaries in this area have no logical basis and in practice the area covered by this book, which offers the walker a great variety of attractive countryside to explore, is divided into two distinct parts both by its natural geography and the influence of man, the dividing line being the M1 and Luton and Dunstable conurbation. To the southwest of this line the hills are traversed by the River Colne and its tributaries, the Ver, Gade, Bulbourne and Chess, which flow southwards to join the Thames in Staines to the west of London, whereas to the northeast of it, the River Lea which rises in Luton and its tributary, the Mimram flow southeastwards to join the Thames in East London and in the extreme northeast corner, the Hiz and its tributaries, the Oughton and the Purwell, flow northwards into the Ouse.

Within this area to the north and east of Luton, the escarpment, here known as the Barton Hills, includes some of the finest and yet least known downland in the Chilterns, while the interior is dominated by Lilley Bottom, a wide valley resembling Hampden Bottom in Bucks, which becomes the Mimram valley above Whitwell. The hills to the northeast of this valley traversed by a maze of narrow lanes are quiet and well-wooded and so are most inviting for the walker to explore. To the southwest a more open ridge gradually giving way to the gentle rolling hills of Central Hertfordshire separates Lilley Bottom from Luton and the Lea valley.

South of the Luton conurbation the first ridge separating the Lea and Ver valleys and climbing to the lofty heights of Blow's Down is generally open in nature and has suffered somewhat from insensitive development. The next ridge, however, between the Ver and Gade valleys dropping gently from the mighty Dunstable Downs to Hemel Hempstead and the M1, and the Gade valley above Hemel have been largely spared the scourge of modern development and with their scattering of woods and remote rural atmosphere offer an expanse of fine walking country. Between the Gade and Bulbourne valleys is a ridge dominated by the Ashridge Estate which rises to the Ivinghoe Hills and with its mixture of copious woodland, picturesque villages and lofty downs is probably the most popular walking area in this book. South of the Bulbourne valley, where the Grand Union Canal towpath and Tring Reservoirs provide pleasant waterside walks, is a range of hills straddled by the Bucks. boundary and the Chess valley, probably the most attractive valley in the northern Chilterns, while finally to the south of Rickmansworth the Colne valley and hills on the former Middlesex border offer surprisingly rural walks with fine views within twenty miles of Central London.

The majority of walks included in this book are in the 5–7 mile range which is justifiably popular for half-day walks, but, for the less energetic or for short winter afternoons, a few shorter versions are indicated in the text, while others can be devised with the assistance of a map. In addition, a number of walks in the 7–11 mile range are included for those preferring a leisurely day's walk or for longer spring and summer afternoons, while a list of possible combinations of walks is provided for those favouring a full day's walk of up to 23 miles.

Details of how to reach the starting points by car are given in the introductory information to each walk and any convenient railway stations are shown on the accompanying plan. Information on bus routes and operators can be obtained by telephoning 0870 – 608 2608.

All the walks described here follow public rights of way, use recognised permissive paths or cross public open space. As the majority of walks cross land used for economic purposes such as agriculture, forestry or the rearing of game, walkers are urged to follow the Country Code at all times:

- Guard against all risk of fire
- Fasten all gates
- Keep dogs under proper control
- Keep to the paths across farmland
- Avoid damaging fences, hedges and walls
- Leave no litter – take it home
- Safeguard water supplies
- Protect wild life, wild plants and trees
- Go carefully on country roads on the right-hand side facing oncoming traffic
- Respect the life of the countryside

Observing these rules helps prevent financial loss to landowners and damage to the environment, as well as the all-too-frequent and sometimes justified bad feeling towards walkers in the countryside.

While it is hoped that the special maps provided with each walk will assist the user to complete the walks without going astray and skeleton details of the surrounding road network are given to enable walkers to shorten the routes in emergency, it is always advisable to take an Ordnance Survey or Chiltern Society map with you to enable you to shorten or otherwise vary the routes without using roads or get your bearings if you do become seriously lost. Details of the appropriate maps are given in the introductory information of each walk.

As for other equipment, readers are advised that some mud will normally be encountered on most walks particularly in woodland except in the driest weather. However proper walking boots are to be recommended at all times as, even when there are no mud problems, hard ruts or rough surfaces make the protection given by boots to the ankles desirable. In addition, the nature of the countryside makes many Chiltern paths prone to overgrowth, particularly in summer. To avoid resultant discomfort, protective clothing is advisable, especially where specific warnings are given.

Some of the walks may be familiar to readers as they were previously published in 'Walks in the Hertfordshire Chilterns' or 'Walks for Motorists : Chilterns (Northern Area)' which are now out of print, but more than half are completely new or have been radically altered, while all of the old walks have been rechecked and brought up to date. In addition, as the walks are appearing in the Chiltern Society's name, all the path numbers have been shown on the plans and incorporated into the texts. These numbers, which are also shown on the Society's Footpath Maps (where available), consist of the official County Council footpath number with the prefix letters used by the Society to indicate the parish concerned. It is therefore most helpful to use these when reporting any path problems you may find, together, if possible, with the national grid reference for the precise location of the trouble spot, as, in this way, the problem can be identified on the ground with a minimum of loss of time in looking for it. National grid references can, however, only be calculated with the help of Ordnance Survey Landranger, Explorer or Pathfinder maps and an explanation of how this is done can be found in the Key to all Landranger or Explorer maps.

The length of time required for any particular walk depends on a number of factors such as your personal walking speed, the number of hills, stiles, etc. to be negotiated, whether or not you stop to rest, eat or drink, investigate places of interest, etc. and the number of impediments such as mud, crops, overgrowth, ploughing, etc. which you encounter, but generally an average speed of between two and two and a half miles per hour is about right in the Chilterns. It is, however, always advisable to allow extra time if you are limited by the daylight or catching a particular bus or train home in order to avoid your walk developing into a race against the clock.

Should you have problems with any of the paths used on the walks or find that the description given is no longer correct, the author would be most grateful if you could let him have details (c/o The Book Castle), so that attempts can be made to rectify the problem or the text can be corrected at the next reprint. Nevertheless, the author hopes that you will not encounter any serious problems and have pleasure from following the walks.

The Chiltern Society was founded in 1965 with the objects: 'To encourage high standards of town and country planning and architecture and to stimulate public interest in and care for the beauty, history and character of the area of the Chiltern Hills.'

The Society Rights of Way Group actively protects and restores public rights of way in the Chilterns – some 5,000 paths. It has surveyed every individual path and takes up irregularities with local parish councils, district or county councils to preserve public rights. It organises voluntary working parties most weekends to clear, waymark or otherwise encourage the use of paths for the public to enjoy the Chiltern countryside. Details of the Society's activities and footpath maps as well as membership application forms can be obtained from the Administrator:

The Chiltern Society
White Hill Centre
White Hill
Chesham
Buckinghamshire HP5 1AG

Tel/Fax: 01494 771250

E-mail: chiltern,society@cwcom.net
Website: www.chilternsociety.freeserve.co.uk

9

INDEX MAP

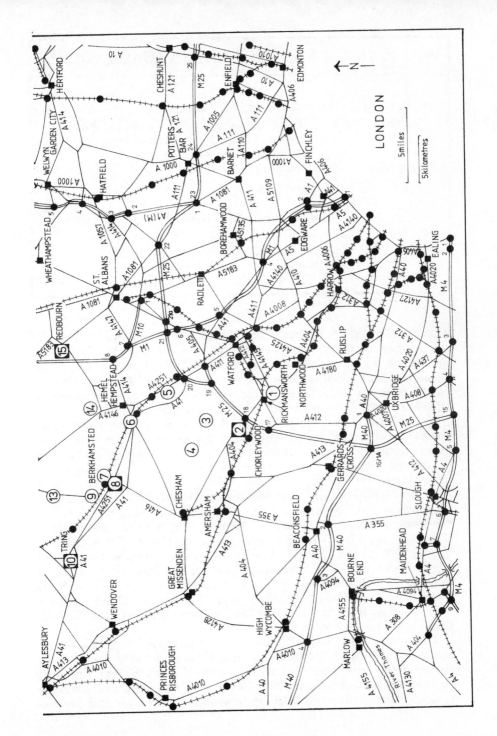

11

WALK 1: Rickmansworth (Batchworth)

Length of Walk: 7.1 miles / 11.4 Km

Starting Point: Roundabout at the junction of the A404 and A4145 at Batchworth on the edge of Rickmansworth.

Grid Ref: TQ064939

Maps: OS Landranger Sheet 176
OS Explorer Sheet 172
OS Pathfinder Sheet 1139 (TQ09/19)

Parking: Cars can be parked in the service road alongside the A4145 (Moor Lane) at its junction with the A404. Access to this service road can be obtained from the roundabout.

Rickmansworth, familiarly known as 'Ricky', is situated at the confluence of three Chiltern rivers, the Colne, the Gade and the Chess. These waterways together with the presence of two ancient parks close to the town have ensured that its setting has remained relatively rural despite the rapid expansion which resulted from the coming of the Metropolitan Line in 1887. Indeed if one visits the old town centre with its narrow streets, which through-traffic now bypasses, it still retains its quiet country town atmosphere, even if the genuine old buildings have been supplemented by a number of modern imitations. The parish church, which was largely rebuilt in 1826 and 1890, retains its old tower dating from 1630 and a number of old brasses and monuments including the tomb of Sir Robert Carey, first Earl of Monmouth, who in 1603 rode to Holyrood to inform King James VI of Scotland of the death of Queen Elizabeth I and his consequent succession to the English throne. Other famous names associated with the town include Cardinal Wolsey, who owned Moor Park, William Penn, the prominent Quaker and founder of Pennsylvania, who lived at Basing House in the 1670s and the writer, George Eliot, who also lived in the town.

The walk, which is of a fairly easy nature, soon leaves the town behind and follows the Grand Union Canal towpath in its surprisingly rural setting to Springwell Lock before crossing the canal and continuing parallel to it to the edge of Harefield. It then climbs through a bluebell wood to Hill End and crosses the hills to Woodcock Hill and Batchworth Heath with fine views at a number of points, before returning across Moor Park Golf Course with its splendid mansion to your point of departure.

Starting from the roundabout at the junction of the A404 and A4145 at Batchworth on the edge of Rickmansworth, follow the right-hand pavement of the A404 towards Rickmansworth for some 300 yards. After crossing the bridge over the Grand Union Canal, by Batchworth Lock House, turn right down a flight of steps to reach the canal towpath at Batchworth Lock. Here turn right passing under the A404 bridge and following the towpath straight on, soon leaving the town behind. After three-quarters of a mile, on reaching Stocker's Lock, to your left is Stocker's Farm which became famous as the set for the TV series of 'Black Beauty'. Just past the lock, go under a hump-backed bridge and continue to follow the towpath (later on path U7) for a further two-thirds of a mile, at one point passing a large boundary stone marking the boundary of Hertfordshire and the former county of Middlesex and then a derelict cement works.

On nearing Springwell Lock leave the towpath and join Springwell Lane to your right. Just past the lock follow the road turning left over Bridge No. 176, then turning right and climbing gently past a number of cottages with views of Springwell Lake, a flooded former gravel pit, to your right. Having passed the cottages, at a sharp left-hand bend where a right-hand crash-barrier ends, fork right onto fenced path U4. Having crossed a stile, join a hard track and follow it downhill to a barn. Here turn left and take a track gently uphill with wide views across the Colne valley towards the distant M25 opening out to your right. Just beyond some farm buildings, where the track bears left, leave it and take path U8 straight on along a fenced path right of a gate to reach a bridlegate. Now take a gravel path straight on beside a right-hand fence, later a hedge, to the far end of the field. Here go through a bridlegate right of two gates, ignore a gate to your right and follow an enclosed path to another bridlegate where the path bears right downhill, with an old gravel pit now used as a firing range to your left. At the bottom ignore a stile to your left and go through another gate, then continue through scrubland between the quarry and the canal bank eventually reaching the quarry entrance. Here turn right onto a track, soon passing a padlocked gate to enter a factory car park on the edge of Harefield.

Go straight on through the car park to join a road called Summerhouse Lane, then follow it straight on between factories, soon rejoining the canal bank. Where further factories commence to your right, turn left onto a macadam footway beside a concrete road (path U9). On reaching some terraced cottages, where the road and footway bear right, cross the road and take an access road straight on uphill passing the cottages and a smallholding. At the entrance to Parkwood Farm Kennels, leave the road and go straight on between anti-horse barriers into a fenced path which climbs through Park Wood, in early May a mass of bluebells. At the top of the hill, cross a footbridge over a spring, then take the fenced path straight on between fields to a road at Hill End.

Cross this road and turn left along its pavement, then opposite a large pond concealed by willow trees turn right onto path U2, an access road to a number of houses. At the far end of this road go straight on over a stile into a field, then bear slightly left following a worn path beside a depression in the ground across the field to cross a stile. Here bear slightly left and follow a left-hand hedge. Where the hedge bears left, leave it and go straight on to cross a stile under a tree in a corner of the field. Now follow a left-hand hedge straight on downhill to a stile and footbridge, then follow a crop break straight on uphill to cross a stile at the county boundary. Here take path RK58 beside a left-hand hedge to Fieldways Farm where you join the farm drive and follow it straight on. Just before reaching Harefield Road, turn sharp right through a fence gap onto path RK57 crossing a field diagonally to pass just left of a telegraph pole and cross a stile just left of the far corner of the field. Now bear half right across the corner of the next field to cross a stile by a white gate, then cross a further field diagonally to a stile in the far corner leading to Harefield Road opposite a county boundary stone.

Turn left onto this road, then at a road junction by the 'Rose and Crown' at Woodcock Hill turn left. Opposite the pub car park turn right onto fenced path RK55. Where this emerges over low rails into a field with fine views ahead towards Batchworth Heath, go straight on downhill to a hedge gap in the bottom corner, then follow the outside edge of a wood called Long Spring downhill. At the bottom of the hill, leave the right-hand hedge and go straight on across the field to cross a stile in the far corner. Now turn right and follow a right-hand hedge along the edge of a golf course, ignoring a redundant stile. By an iron gate and redundant stile step, enter a fenced path and follow it uphill to reach a layby on the A404 at Batchworth Heath Hill. Turn right into the layby and where it ends, cross the A404, turn right onto its pavement and follow it downhill and up again to Batchworth Heath.

At the top of the hill turn left into Park Close. Where the road turns right, leave it and take enclosed path RK54 straight on between private drives, soon emerging onto Moor Park Golf Course. Here go straight on, following a series of four-foot wooden marker posts with white arrows passing left of a small lake and crossing several

WALK 1

15

fairways. Having traversed a small copse, there is a fine view to your right of Moor Park mansion. Described by Sir Niklaus Pevsner as 'the grandest eighteenth-century mansion in Hertfordshire', Moor Park is, in fact, a seventeenth-century house which was remodelled in the Palladian style for the merchant Benjamin Styles by the architect Sir James Thornhill between 1725 and 1727 with a rich rococo interior and a large classical portico. The house, which had, before its remodelling, been the home of the ill-fated Duke of Monmouth, was acquired by Rickmansworth UDC in 1937 and is now almost certainly the most magnificent golf clubhouse in the country.

Continue to follow the marker posts straight on, passing a bench, then right of a copse, then left of a second copse to join a macadam drive by a gnarled oak tree. Follow this drive for about 50 yards then fork right, following the marker posts diagonally across a fairway, then bearing slightly left to pass through a gap in a tree belt and continue downhill to rejoin the macadam drive. Turn right onto this and follow it past the 'Fairway Inn' and on to the A4145. Cross this road carefully, then turn left for your starting point.

WALK 2:   Chorleywood

Length of Walk: (A) 6.9 miles / 11.1 Km
                           (B) 5.8 miles / 9.3 Km

Starting Point: Car park on south side of A404 by
Chorleywood Cricket Pavilion.

Grid Ref: TQ034967

Maps: OS Landranger Sheets 166 or 176
OS Explorer Sheet 172
OS Pathfinder Sheet 1139 (TQ09/19)
Chiltern Society FP Map No. 5

How to get there / Parking: Chorleywood, 2 miles northwest
of Rickmansworth, may be reached by leaving the M25 at
Junction 18 and taking the A404 towards Amersham.
Having passed Chorleywood Church on your left, the car
park by the cricket pavilion is some 300 yards beyond on
your left.

Notes: Heavy nettle growth may be encountered at several
points on both walks in the summer months, while
bridleway CN3 is prone to deep mud in places, even in
dry weather.

Chorleywood, with its 200-acres partially wooded common, is
perhaps a typical example of the curious mixture of
countryside and suburbia found in what was once called
'Metroland'. To the east and west of the common are sizeable
built-up areas which have grown up since the Metropolitan
Railway reached the village in 1889, while the spacious
common itself is surrounded by typical Chiltern cottages and
on the edge of the village is the farmhouse where the Quaker,
William Penn, who later founded the American state of
Pennsylvania, was married in 1672.

Both walks first lead you across the common to the built-up
area around Chorleywood Station before leaving the village
and passing through pleasant beechwoods and a long green
lane to the outskirts of Chenies. Here Walk B leads you
through the village before dropping into the Chess valley at
Sarratt Bottom, while Walk A makes a gradual and scenic
descent into the Chess valley at the picture-book village of
Latimer. It then turns to follow the Chess valley downstream

WALK 2

18

past the ruins of the old Flaunden Church as well as Dodds Mill to rejoin Walk B. Both walks then climb to Sarratt Church before returning across the Chess valley and through Chorleywood Park to your starting point.

Both walks start from the car park by Chorleywood Cricket Pavilion on the south side of the A404 and take path CW32b, a wide glade leading from the rear of the car park across the wooded common. On emerging from the trees, go straight on until you reach a worn crossing path. Turn left onto this path, which is later marked as a 'horse track' and follow it, ignoring a fork to the left at one point, until you reach Common Road at a gap in the houses by a bus stop left of the 'Rose and Crown'. Cross the road here and take path CW15, a macadam lane called Colley Land, straight on downhill. This later narrows to a path and reaches another road by the Metropolitan Line embankment. Turn right onto this road then immediately left under a railway bridge. At a crossroads by a shopping parade, turn right and at a fork, go right again into the continuation of Whitelands Avenue. Ignore two branching roads to the left, then between 59 and 61 Whitelands Avenue, turn left onto fenced path CW–CN2 passing through a squeeze-stile and taking the path into Carpenter's Wood.

On reaching the wood, turn immediately right and follow back garden fences along the edge of the wood. Where the gardens end, go straight on through Whitelands Wood, soon walking parallel to and later joining a permissive bridleway. At the far side of the wood turn right onto bridleway CN3 joining the Chiltern Way and passing either side of a gate then under a railway bridge. Now take a hedged green lane straight on for over half a mile, passing through Halsey's Wood and eventually reaching the A404 at Chenies Turn. Here cross the A404 and leaving the Chiltern Way, turn left onto its pavement, following it for some 200 yards, then turn right onto path CN34, the rough drive to Great House Farm, with wide views of the Chess valley to your left and of Chenies Manor House, rebuilt by the first Earl of Bedford in 1530, and the outskirts of the village to your right.

On reaching a fork, Walk B turns right onto bridleway CN35 and follows this, then the village street, straight on to the picturesque village green. Here, at a fork, leave the road and bear half right across the green heading for a macadam lane left of a white cottage with lattice windows where you join Walk 4A. Now see the text of Walk 4.

At the junction of CN34/CN35, Walk 2A takes bridleway CN35 straight on to the start of a left-hand copse. Here turn left onto path CN48, the drive to 'The Farm House', then turning immediately right over a stile. Now follow an obvious path through the copse to a stile. Cross this, a farm road and another stile opposite and take path CN42 straight on through a wood. At a fork bear left to cross a stile at the edge of the wood with a fine view of Latimer nestling in the Chess valley ahead. Here turn right over a second stile, then turn left and gradually diverge from the left-hand fence to cross a further stile. Now go straight on across the next field to reach the top corner of Coney Wood. Here follow the top edge of this wood, later a right-hand hedge to enter a corner of Walk Wood. Just inside the wood, turn right over a stile where you obtain a fine view of Latimer and the Chess valley with Latimer House partially hidden in trees on the wooded hill to your left.

Latimer, until the nineteenth century variously known as 'Isenhampstead Cheynduit' or 'Isenhampstead Latimer', was formerly a hamlet of Chesham belonging to the Cavendish family (later the Lords Chesham) of Latimer House. The original house, where Charles I was held prisoner in 1647, was largely rebuilt in the nineteenth century in neo-Tudor style. The village church was also rebuilt in 1841 and renovated by Sir George Gilbert Scott in 1867, while many of the picturesque village cottages also date from this period.

Now bear half left across the field to a stile in the bottom left-hand corner leading to a crossroads. Cross the stile and the major road and take the road signposted to Latimer and Flaunden straight on to a bridge over the River Chess by a weir. At the far end of the bridge, turn right over a stile by a green gate onto path LT20 and follow a right-hand fence at first, then bear slightly right to cross a culvert. Now follow a right-hand fence (soon on bridleway CN56) eventually passing a clump of trees to your right which conceals the ruins of the old Flaunden church. This thirteenth-century church was abandoned in 1838 when a new church was built in the hilltop village of Flaunden more than a mile away. Although the old church was still used for occasional services, it was already a ruin by the late nineteenth century and very little of it now remains. On reaching a gate and stile at the far left-hand corner of the field, cross the stile and follow a left-hand fence to an old tomb shaded by two oaks. Here go straight on for a third of a mile, soon passing through a gate and continuing to Mill Farm at Chenies Bottom (where home-made ice-cream is on sale), then go straight on through the farmyard to a road near Dodds Mill.

Walks 2A and 4B turn left onto the road and follow it to a left-hand bend. Here leave the road and take path CN60 straight on over a stile by a gate then along the top of a slight bank marking the edge of the flood plain. Having crossed a stile, go straight on, crossing another stile at the far side of the field and following a left-hand hedge to a stile into Limeshill Wood. Now take path SA37 straight on through the wood then take a fenced path, soon bearing right then left and later crossing a stile. Eventually you cross another stile leading to a junction of concrete roads by a ford and footbridge over the Chess, where **Walk 4B** turns left onto path SA36 rejoining **Walk 4A** (now return to the text of **Walk** 4), while **Walk 2A** takes path SA37 straight on rejoining **Walk 2B**.

Walks 2A and 2B now follow the concrete road straight on for a quarter mile to a bend in a road by some cottages at Sarratt Bottom. Turn right onto this road and at a junction turn left past a white cottage. Some 50 yards beyond the cottage, turn right through a kissing-gate onto path SA39 and follow a right-hand hedge to a stile. Cross this and bear slightly left across a field to the far left-hand corner. Here ignore a stile to your left and bear slightly right into a tree-lined lane, following this uphill. Near the top, take the Chiltern Way straight on over a stile by a gate into a field and follow its right-hand hedge. At the far side of the field leaving the Chiltern Way, bear half right over a stile and through a kissing-gate into Sarratt churchyard (briefly joining **Walk 3**) and take a gravel path passing right of the twelfth-century church (described in the introduction to Walk 3).

At a fork in the path, go right (leaving **Walk 3** again), passing through a handgate and taking path SA40 straight on through a kissing-gate. Now follow a left-hand fence then a right-hand hedge to the macadam drive to an early nineteenth-century manor house called Goldingtons. Cross the drive and a stile, with a fine view of the Chess valley ahead, and follow a right-hand fence straight on downhill to cross a stile near a cottage and join its drive. Now follow this, turning left onto path SA41 to reach a road. Cross this and go through a kissing-gate opposite, then follow a right-hand hedge straight on to the far end of the field. Here go straight on through a fence gap then turn right into a thicket and follow a left-hand fence beside a poplar copse to a footbridge over a very picturesque section of the River Chess. Just beyond the end of this footbridge, turn left through a kissing-gate onto path CW2 into a belt of trees. Disregarding a fork to the left, take an obvious path straight on for about 350 yards to a T-junction of paths at the far end of the tree-belt. Here turn right over a stile onto path CW34 into a wood and follow a well-defined path uphill, eventually joining a track which soon enters an avenue of trees in Chorleywood Park. Follow this avenue to its far end, then at a junction of tracks, turn right. On reaching a macadam drive, turn left onto it and follow it, with Chorleywood House soon coming into view to your right, until you reach gates leading to the A404 directly opposite your starting point.

WALK 3:   Sarratt

Length of Walk: 6.3 miles / 10.1 Km

Starting Point: 'The Boot', Sarratt Green.

Grid Ref: TQ042996

Maps: OS Landranger Sheets 166 or 176
OS Explorer Sheet 172
OS Pathfinder Sheet 1139 (TQ09/19)
(part only) Chiltern Society FP Map No. 5

How to get there / Parking: Sarratt Green, 3.5 miles north of Rickmansworth, may be reached by leaving the M25 at Junction 18 and taking the A404 towards Amersham. After 1 mile turn right onto a road signposted to Sarratt and follow it for 1.6 miles to a crossroads near the 'Cricketers' at Sarratt Green. Here turn left and find a suitable parking space along the quiet service road on the left side of the village green.

Notes: Heavy nettle growth may be encountered at several points in the summer months and part of path SA24 is prone to deep mud even in dry weather.

Sarratt, despite its close proximity to the M25 and the large built-up areas of Watford and Rickmansworth, has a remarkably rural setting. The traditional Chiltern cottages of what is now the main village at Sarratt Green are ranged around an attractive and unusually long green with a duckpond at one end, while the ancient village known as Church End about two-thirds of a mile away on the northern slopes of the Chess valley now has little more than the church, a pub, a nineteenth-century manor house and some almshouses rebuilt in the same period. The cruciform twelfth-century church, appropriately dedicated to the Holy Cross, is particularly interesting as its tower was rebuilt in the fifteenth century in part with Roman bricks (presumably emanating from the ruins of a Roman villa discovered in the vicinity) and it is also the only church tower in Hertfordshire to have a saddleback roof. The church, restored by Sir George Gilbert Scott in 1865, also contains a Norman font, a fragment of a thirteenth-century wall-painting and a carved Jacobean pulpit, from which the renowned Nonconformist Richard Baxter preached in the seventeenth century.

The walk, which explores the surprisingly remote hilltop plateau between Watford and the Chess valley with its bluebell woods, leads you from Sarratt Green via the wooded Dawes Common to Church End, near which fine views open out from time to time across the Chess valley. It then takes you over the M25 and via Micklefield Hall to the edge of Croxley Green, before returning by way of Chandler's Cross to Sarratt Green.

Starting from the 'Boot' pub on the northeast side of Sarratt Green, take the road along the edge of the green northwestwards to its junction with the road to Commonwood, then bear half left across the green, passing left of a pond to reach a path signposted to Dawes Lane (SA27). Take this path along a gravel lane, ignoring branching drives to your right, to cross a stile by a gate at the far end. Now bear slightly right across a field to the corner of a hedge ahead, then follow the left-hand hedge until it turns left. Here bear half left across the field to cross a stile in the field corner into the wooded Dawes Common. In the wood, take a gravel track (path SA52) straight on, soon swinging left by a right-hand gate and kissing-gate onto path SA24, joining the Chiltern Way to reach Dawes Lane.

Cross this road and go through a kissing-gate by a gate opposite and take path SA24 straight on through woodland, soon passing between fenced plantations then entering mature woodland. Now at a fork take the right-hand option which soon passes through a kissing-gate and follows a right-hand hedge along the edge of Sandfield Wood to a further kissing-gate by a house leading onto a gravel track. Take this track straight on along the edge of the wood, ignoring a crossing track, then at a left-hand bend, take path SA24 straight on through another kissing-gate and over a stile and follow the edge of a left-hand wood with fine views of the Chess valley to your right. At a corner of the wood go straight on across a field, with Sarratt Church soon coming into view ahead, to reach a stile and kissing-gate into the churchyard. Leaving the Chiltern Way and briefly joining **Walk 2**, in the churchyard follow a gravel path passing right of the church.

At a fork in the path keep left, leaving **Walk 2** and going through a lychgate into Church Lane. Turn right onto this road and follow it round a left-hand bend. At a sharp right-hand bend leave the road and take path SA33 straight on over a stile by a gate. Now follow the edge of a wood downhill with a view to your right across the Chess valley to Chorleywood. At the bottom corner of the field, turn right then after a few yards turn left through some iron railings and over a stile. Here bear half right across a field, climbing to a hedge gap just right of the right-hand of two oaks ahead. Now go straight on across the next field to a hedge gap right of New Model Farm. Go straight on across the next field to join a left-hand hedge at a slight bend in it then follow this hedge downhill to a bridge over the M25. At the far end of the bridge, take a track straight on beside a left-hand hedge for a quarter mile, eventually reaching Solesbridge Lane by New Cottages.

Cross this road and take path SA45, a rough track, straight on, passing through a gap by a padlocked gate by a new house leading to a concreted farmyard at Micklefield Hall. Go straight on through the farmyard, then turn left onto a concrete farm road. Now turn right into a hedged lane (still SA45) and follow it straight on for a third of a mile, soon entering a wood called Round Spring where you ignore the two right-hand branching tracks into the wood. On leaving the wood and emerging into a field, follow a right-hand tree-belt straight on to its end. Here bear half left across the field to a stile. Cross this and bear slightly right onto path SA47 following a right-hand hedge to cross another stile at the far end of the field. Now take path SA46 straight on across the next field to a further stile, then bear half left across another field to a stile left of a flagpole leading into a garden. Here go straight on keeping left of an ornamental hedge to reach a roadside hedge, then follow this hedge, later joining a macadam drive to reach a bend in Sarratt Road. Now take this road straight on to its junction with Little Green Lane on the edge of Croxley Green.

Here turn left onto path SA15, a rough farm road and follow it beside a left-hand hedge for a quarter mile. At a crossways go straight on, then ignore a signposted path to the right and bear slightly left into a hedged lane. On reaching a timber-framed single-storey cottage, take a narrow hedged path straight on. This becomes a fenced path along the edge of a field and ultimately reaches a stile into Harrocks Wood. Follow an obvious path straight on through this wood and at the far side of the wood go straight on through a squeeze-stile and take a fenced path to a kissing-gate leading to a road junction by the 'Clarendon Arms' at Chandler's Cross.

Here cross the major road and take Chandler's Lane straight on uphill for half a mile, recrossing the M25 and passing Potten Farm and Yew Court Farm with its attractive timber buildings and courtyard. At the junction with Templepan Lane, turn left through a kissing-gate onto path SA13 and cross a field diagonally heading for the left-hand end of a copse. On reaching the copse, follow its edge to a macadam farm road, then turn left onto it and follow it to Newhall Farm. Here turn left by a black barn, keeping the barn to your right, then at the far end of the barn, turn right onto a concrete farm road between the barn and a left-hand tractor shed. Follow this concrete road (still SA13) straight on, leaving the farm and after nearly half a

WALK 3

N

M 25 sth Jnr

M 25

Jct. 19

CHANDLER'S CROSS

Great Westwood

Templeman Lane

Yew Court Farm

Patten Chandlers Lane
Farm

"Clarendon Arms"

SA15

SA13

Newhall
Farm

SA13

Deadman's Ash
Mill

SA48

SA48
'Boot'

Start

SARRATT
'Cricketers'

SA 27

SA24

Dawes Lane

Sandfield
Wood

Chiltern Way
Dawes Common

SA62
SA39

Church Lane

Chiltern Way/
Walk 2
Goldingtons

SA SA
124

SARRATT
(CHURCH END)

'Cock'

SA40
Walk 2

SA
33

New Model
Farm

SA
33

New
Cottages
SA 45

Scatterdells Lane

M 25

Micklefield
Hall

Round
Spring

Model
Farm

SA45

SA47
SA
46

Sarratt Road

Harrocks
Wood

SA
15

Little Green Lane

CROXLEY
GREEN

CHORLEYWOOD

1mile

1 kilometre

0   0

25

mile reaching a road at Sarratt called Deadman's Ash Hill. Turn left onto this road and follow it for about 100 yards, then at the end of a right-hand hedge, turn right onto the macadam drive to numbers 1 to 4 The Old Cottages. Where this drive forks, cross a stile in the middle of the fork and take fenced path SA48 straight on to a kissing-gate at the far end of the right-hand garden. Here go straight on across two paddocks to a kissing-gate in the far corner of the second. Now follow the left-hand fence of a tree nursery straight on. Where it bears left, keep straight on across the field to a kissing-gate by the far hedge into a fenced path which leads you out to Sarratt Green near the 'Boot'.

WALK 4: Flaunden

Length of Walk: (A)   6.5 miles / 10.5 Km
                       (B)   6.0 miles / 9.6 Km

Starting Point: Flaunden village crossroads.

Grid Ref: TL016009

Maps: OS Landranger Sheet 166
        OS Explorer Sheets 172 & 182
        OS Pathfinder Sheets 1119 (TL00/10) & 1139 (TQ09/19)
        Chiltern Society FP Map No. 5

How to get there / Parking: Flaunden, 5 miles northwest
of Rickmansworth, may be reached by leaving the M25 at
Junction 18 and taking the A404 through Chorleywood
towards Amersham. After 1.6 miles turn right onto a road
signposted to Chenies and Latimer and follow its winding
course for 1.5 miles passing through Chenies and
descending into the Chess valley. At a crossroads turn
right onto the Latimer and Flaunden road and follow it
straight on for 2 miles to reach Flaunden. Here ignore a
branching road to the right and pass the 'Green Dragon',
then either find a suitable place to park where the road
widens out near a telephone box taking care not to
obstruct or park opposite driveways, or, alternatively,
turn left at the crossroads towards Bovingdon and find a
suitable parking place on that road.

Notes: Both alternative walks are prone to heavy nettle
growth in summer and deep mud in places even in dry
weather.

Flaunden, locally pronounced 'Flarnden', is an unspoilt
secluded village clustered around a crossroads of narrow
lanes on a hilltop north of the Chess valley. The village church,
built in 1838 to replace a thirteenth-century predecessor over
a mile away in the Chess valley, is notable for being the first to
be designed by the celebrated architect, Sir George Gilbert
Scott, who was later responsible for the Midland Grand Hotel
in London which forms the façade of St. Pancras Station. This
church incorporates several items from its predecessor
including its fifteenth-century font, three ancient bells and the
one-handed church clock.

WALK 4

CHIPPERFIELD

FLAUNDEN

BELSIZE

CHENIES BOTTOM

CHENIES

N

0   1 mile

0   1 kilometre

28

Both walks, which are characterised by a mixture of fine views and pleasant woodland, lead you down into the idyllically rural Chess valley at Chenies Bottom, where Walk B follows the valley bottom, while Walk A crosses into Bucks. and climbs a wooded hillside to visit the picturesque feudal village of Chenies. After Walk A drops again to rejoin Walk B, both routes return to Flaunden by way of the quiet hamlet of Belsize nestling in a Chiltern hollow.

Both walks start from Flaunden village crossroads and take the road signposted to Latimer and Chesham. Go past the 'Green Dragon' then at a road junction by the church, fork left into a cul-de-sac road (joining the reverse direction of Bucks. Walk 8) and follow it for nearly half a mile to a fork by wooden gates. Here fork left onto hedged bridleway FD8 (leaving Bucks. Walk 8 again). After some 25 yards turn right over a stile and take path FD2 beside a left-hand hedge to cross a stile at Martin Top Farm.

Now turn left onto bridleway FD6 between the farm buildings, crossing a concrete road and taking a fenced bridleway straight on across a field. At the far side of the field follow the bridleway turning right to reach a concrete farm road. Now take path FD2a straight on over a stile following a right-hand fence, later the outside edge of Baldwin's Wood, gradually descending with views of the Chess valley ahead and Sarratt Church and Goldingtons on a hilltop to your left, to reach a crossing track. Cross this and a stile with wide views of the Chess valley opening out ahead, then take path CN59 straight on downhill, passing just left of an oak tree to reach two stiles leading into a farmyard at Mill Farm. Now go straight on through the farmyard to a gate onto the road in Chenies Bottom, where you meet Walk 2A. (NB. Home-made ice-cream is sold at the farm!)

Walk B turns left here onto the road joining Walk 2A. Now see the text of Walk 2. Walk A bears slightly right onto the road crossing two bridges over arms of the Chess and passing Dodd's Mill, then where the road forks, keep right. At a T-junction, cross the major road and take path CN37 into the wood opposite. Just inside the wood, fork left and take a winding path uphill ignoring branching paths to your right to cross a stile. Now take a hedged, later walled path uphill past Chenies Church to the gates of Chenies Manor House. The church to your left dates from the fifteenth century and is principally notable for the Russell family chapel which was added a century later and houses numerous monuments to the Earls and Dukes of Bedford and other members of the Russell family. The Manor to your right was rebuilt by the first Earl of Bedford in 1530 and was, at one time, known as Chenies Palace, possibly due to both Henry VIII and Elizabeth I staying there several times. The village, whose name derives from the Cheynes family, from whom it passed to the Russells by female succession in 1526, was originally known as Isenhampstead and then Isenhampstead Cheynes. Its name only contracted to its present form in the nineteenth century when a benevolent Duke of Bedford also had many of its cottages rebuilt or improved.

By the Manor gates turn left down the drive to the picturesque village green. At a crossways, bear slightly left across the green heading for a macadam lane left of a white cottage. Here **Walks 2B and 4A** cross the major road and follow the lane (path CN16) straight on out of the village for nearly half a mile, at one point passing through gates. On reaching Mountwood Farm, by some wooden rails fork right onto a fenced grassy path swinging left. Where this path joins a stony track, turn immediately left over a stile onto path CN19 and bear slightly right across a field to a stile into Mount Wood. In the wood take a waymarked path straight on until you reach a stile. Cross this and continue downhill through a plantation to reach a track by a gate and stile. Turn left over the stile and go straight on to a gap by a white gate into Holloway Lane then turn right onto this road to reach a ford and footbridge over the Chess. Cross the bridge and a stile, then **Walk 2B** turns right onto a farm road (path SA37) rejoining Walk 2A (now see text of Walk 2); while **Walk 4A** rejoins **Walk 4B** taking path SA36 straight on along the farm road.

At Valley Farm **Walks 4A and 4B** fork right by an oak tree following a right-hand fence to a gate into a hedged path. Take this path straight on, crossing a stile at one point, then ignore a crossing path and bear slightly left over a stile into the continuation of the hedged path leading to a stile into Hanginglane Wood. Here take the obvious path straight on through the wood to its far side. Now ignore a crossing track and take a stony track straight on through a tree belt. At the far end of the tree belt you currently have to take a *de facto* route continuing along the track to a T-junction with a concrete road near Rosehall Farm where you rejoin the official right of way.

Turn right onto this road (path SA25) and where its concrete surface ends, fork right onto a farm road soon passing Rosehall Wood. At the far side of the wood, where the farm road turns left, leave it, forking right over a stile between a gate and an oak tree and heading for a house visible through a hedge gap right of a pylon to cross a stile in the next hedge. Now bear half left to a gate by the corner of a hedge then bear half left again to a stile just right of some power-lines. Cross this and turn left onto a road. Just past a cottage, turn right through a hedge gap into Plough Wood, then fork immediately left onto waymarked path SA21 and follow it diagonally across the wood, ignoring a crossing track, then crossing a stile into a field corner. Here follow the outside edge of the wood straight on, then at a corner of the wood, bear half right across the field to a stile onto Poles Hill at Belsize.

Cross this road and turn right along its pavement. At a left-hand bend, cross the road again and go straight on across the village green to an entrance left of a telephone box. Here take path SA1, a concreted lane, uphill. Where its concrete surface ends, follow its rough continuation straight on to a fork at the edge of a wood called Penman's Green. Here fork left onto a track into the wood and where it forks, take the lesser right-hand option straight on, soon passing through an anti-horse barrier and joining a gravel drive. Follow this straight on between gateposts, then turn left onto a rough road called Little Windmill Hill which later becomes macadamed and descends to a T-junction.

Here turn right onto the pavement of Dunny Lane and after some 60 yards, turn left crossing the road and passing through a squeeze-stile by a gate onto path SA20 following a right-hand hedge uphill. At the far end of the field, go straight on into a corner of Woodman's Wood and follow its inside edge straight on. Where woodland commences to your right, take the obvious path straight on for about 200 yards ignoring a crossing bridleway. Now, at a fork, bear left, eventually reaching a gate and gap leading to Olleberrie Lane. Turn right onto this road and follow it for some 350 yards, then just past a cottage called Hollow Hedge, joining the Chiltern Way, turn left over a stile by a gate onto path FD14 into a wood called Lower Plantation. Take the obvious path straight on along the inside edge of the wood at first, then through the middle of the wood to reach a stile leading to a road junction. Here take the Flaunden and Chenies road straight on for over a quarter mile to Flaunden crossroads.

WALK 5:   King's Langley

Length of Walk: 6.8 miles / 11.0 Km
Starting Point: Crossroads near King's Langley cricket pitch.
Grid Ref: TL066028
Maps: OS Landranger Sheet 166
           OS Explorer Sheet 182
           OS Pathfinder Sheet 1119 (TL00/10)
           (part only) Chiltern Society FP Map No. 5
How to get there / Parking: King's Langley, 2.5 miles
southeast of Hemel Hempstead, may be reached from the
town by taking the old A4251 towards Watford. In the
village centre, turn right into Vicarage Lane (signposted
to Chipperfield, Sarratt and Bovingdon) and follow it
uphill for 750 yards. Just past the cricket pitch to your
right, turn right at a crossroads into Love Lane, where
there is a parking area on the edge of the common
immediately on your right.

King's Langley, on the western slopes of the Gade valley, now
has its centre along the old A4251 near which can be found the
fifteenth-century parish church. This was, however, not
always the case, as the thirteenth-century royal palace and
early fourteenth-century priory were both situated at the top
of the hill. Indeed, in mediaeval times the village was for more
than two centuries at the centre of the national stage. King's
Langley Palace was built for Queen Eleanor, wife of Edward I,
whose son, later to become Edward II, was brought up here
and as king frequently stayed here. In 1315, Edward II had his
lifelong friend Piers Gaveston buried at the Priory some two
years after the latter had been beheaded by the Earl of
Warwick. Another prominent victim of a violent death to be
buried at the Priory was Richard II, but his remains were later
removed by Henry V for reburial in Westminster Abbey.
Prince Edmund de Langley, the fifth son of Edward III, who
was later made the first Duke of York, was born at the Palace
in 1341 and buried at the Priory in 1402, but when the latter
was suppressed during the Reformation, his remains were
moved to the parish church, where his tomb can still be seen
today. Part of the Palace was destroyed by fire in the fifteenth

century, after which it declined in importance. Today, little remains of this mediaeval royal residence and of the Priory, only one building has survived which is now part of Rudolf Steiner School.

The walk takes you from the attractive common of King's Langley past the sites of the Priory and the Palace across the open, rolling hills southwest of the village to Chipperfield with its wooded common before returning by way of Tower Hill and Shendish to King's Langley.

Starting from the crossroads of Vicarage Lane, Love Lane, Langley Hill and Chipperfield Road, take Langley Hill downhill past the site of the Priory. At a sharp left-hand bend by a pub called the 'Old Palace', turn right; then, by the entrance to Rudolf Steiner School, turn left onto path KL7, a narrow alleyway right of a garage, passing between hedges to a stile. Cross this, with a fine view ahead across the Gade valley spanned by the M25 viaduct to Abbot's Langley and the Colne valley beyond, then go straight on across a field to cross two stiles on the next rise. Now turn right onto path KL8 following a track beside a right-hand fence. Where this track turns right, bear half left to cross a stile then continue across a small plantation to a footbridge over the A41. Cross this bridge then turn left onto path KL5 to cross a stile by a gate. Now bear slightly left across a field to cross a stile left of a small fenced compound. Here bear half right following a left-hand hedge through a plantation to cross a stile, then follow a left-hand fence to a stile into a plantation. Go straight on through the plantation to a stile leading to a junction of concrete roads by the farm.

Take the middle option (path KL3) straight on past a Georgian house, then bearing left between large ponds with an imposing house called Kings Langley Lodge hidden in the trees to your left. By a modern house and farm buildings, turn right, keeping the farm buildings to your left and the house to your right, to leave the farm by way of a stile by a gate. Now take a fenced farm track straight on downhill, ignoring stiles in both fences. At the end of this track, follow a left-hand fence and sporadic hedge virtually straight on downhill to cross a stile in a thick hedge. Now bear half-left uphill across a field to a gate and squeeze-stile at the left-hand end of a clump of trees. Go through the squeeze-stile and turn right onto a sunken track (bridleway SA64). Follow this uphill for about 300 yards, then, after it levels off, at a left-hand bend just short of Jeffrey's Farm, the reputed home of President Jimmy Carter's ancestors, leave the track and take path SA64, heading half-right across a field towards a tall redwood tree on the skyline, joining a left-hand fence to reach the corner of a garden hedge. Here bear half right again to a stile and hedge gap onto a road called Bucks Hill near Chipperfield Common virtually opposite Callipers Lodge.

Cross the stile then do **not** join the road but turn right onto a fenced bridleway behind the roadside hedge. Where this joins the road, turn left across the road onto path CF3, the left-hand of two tracks, following the back of Chipperfield's wooded common until you reach two cottages. Go past the first of these cottages, then, by an old gateway leading to three garages, turn right onto a narrow path into the woods (CF4). At a T-junction of paths, turn left, soon passing a pond to your left and going straight on to reach the Apostles' Pond. This pond is so named because it used to be surrounded by twelve ancient lime trees which had to be replaced by young trees in 1984 which will take some years to mature. Go straight on past this pond, then, at a fork, take the left-hand option. Follow this path straight on through the woods for nearly half a mile, ignoring all crossing paths, until houses come into sight ahead. Here at a fork, take the left-hand option to reach a road at Chipperfield by a signpost just right of the 'Windmill' pub which stands on or near the site of a windmill shown on the 1822 Ordnance Survey map. The village church built in 1837 and the other village pubs can be reached by taking the road to your right.

Cross this road and take the narrow, fenced path CF10 between gardens to a stile into a field. Now go straight on downhill to a gate and stile in front of the last house in a row in Dunny Lane. Bear slightly left across this road to cross another stile by a gate, then follow a right-hand hedge uphill through a field to a derelict kissing gate. Go through this and continue to follow the right-hand hedge, turning left then right. On entering a copse, go straight on through it to a stile at its far side, then follow a right-hand hedge to cross a stile at the far end of the field. Now bear right through a thicket into a wide hedged lane (bridleway CF11), which leads you to a road at the hamlet of Tower Hill.

Turn right along this road and ignore New Road to your left. Just before the 'Boot', turn left into a lane (path CF12, later CF16) and follow it for a third of a mile until you enter a field. Now follow a right-hand hedge straight on. After a quarter mile, where the hedge turns right, follow it joining path CF14. At a corner of the field, cross a stile and follow a fenced path along the edge of Scatterdells Wood, wiggling to the right and soon reaching Scatterdells Lane. Turn left onto this residential road and follow it to its end. Here go straight on over a stile by a gate onto path CF2 into Scatterdells Wood. At a fork just inside the wood, bear right following a flinty track beside a left-hand fence. Where the fence bears away to the left, at a fork keep left and follow a waymarked track straight on, ignoring a crossing

WALK 5

path in a dip, a crossing track beyond it and a track branching to the right. Now cross a stile and take path KL19, bearing half left across a field to a stile into Barnes Lane. Cross this road and a stile opposite and bear half right, heading towards Shendish House hidden in trees on the next hilltop. On reaching a clump of trees right of the A41 bridge over Rucklers Lane, bear slightly left and follow a right-hand hedge, then a fence downhill to a kissing-gate into Rucklers Lane. Turn right onto this road passing under the A41. After about 120 yards, turn left onto the right-hand of two drives (still path KL19) and follow this uphill through a wood. Where the drive forks, take a narrow path straight on to cross a stile into Shendish Park. Now go straight on across a field to reach a belt of trees concealing Shendish House, then turn right and follow the edge of the tree belt, gradually bearing left to reach a corner of the field.

Here turn sharp right onto path KL17, doubling back across the field, with a fine view to your left across the Gade valley including Abbotshill House, now a school, on the other side of the valley, and heading for a gate and stile right of a brick and flint cottage. Cross this stile and take a wide hedged track straight on downhill to cross Rucklers Lane at the bottom. Now follow a right-hand wire-mesh fence straight on uphill through a wood called The Nucket to a stile, then follow a right-hand hedge straight on across a field to a stile leading to Barnes Lane. Cross this road, then go through a hedge gap with a redundant ladder stile opposite and turn immediately left onto a path (still KL17) between the roadside hedge and a school playing field fence. After about 250 yards, turn right, leaving the roadside hedge and continuing to follow the playing field fence for some 350 yards until you emerge at the school entrance. Here turn left onto the school drive, then immediately right into Love Lane and follow it back to your starting point.

WALK 6: Hemel Hempstead Station

Length of Walk: 5.9 miles / 9.5 Km
Starting Point: Forecourt of Hemel Hempstead Station.
Grid Ref: TL043059
Maps: OS Landranger Sheet 166
OS Explorer Sheet 182
OS Pathfinder Sheet 1119 (TL00/10)
Chiltern Society FP Maps Nos. 5 & 20
Parking: Hemel Hempstead Station is located just off the A4251 at Boxmoor about 1 mile southwest of the town centre. At the mini-roundabout by the station, turn off the main road into Fishery Road, crossing Boxmoor Common and the canal bridge by the 'Fishery Inn', then seek an on-street parking space in one of the side streets.

Since the war, Hemel Hempstead, at the confluence of the rivers Gade and Bulbourne, has developed into a large modern town due to its designation in the late 1940s as a 'new town'. Despite this, the surrounding countryside has retained its rural atmosphere and even the town itself is less of a concrete jungle than some of its counterparts, thanks to the preservation of 'green lungs' particularly along the river valleys. Hemel Hempstead also has a long history as its southern part is traversed by a Roman road known as Akeman Street and remains of Roman villas have been found not only here but also in Gadebridge Park to the north of the town centre. In the Middle Ages, Hemel Hempstead must already have been a wealthy market town as is attested by its magnificent twelfth-century church and in the eighteenth and nineteenth centuries, the construction of the Grand Junction Canal, the L&NWR main line to the Midlands and North and several paper mills where modern paper-making methods were pioneered, all to the south of the mediaeval town, caused its expansion southwards.

The walk soon leaves the town behind, climbing the wooded southern slope of the Bulbourne valley to reach Felden and the rural upland plateau beyond, before leading you to Bovingdon Church. The return route then takes you by way of Stoney Lane and the Westbrook Hay golf course with its fine views of the Bulbourne valley, to Bourne End and the Grand

WALK 6

Union Canal at Winkwell Swing Bridge, probably the most picturesque location on the Chilterns section of the canal, before following its towpath back to the railway station.

Starting from the main entrance to Hemel Hempstead Station, turn left out of the station past a small car park to cross the old A4251 just left of a mini-roundabout. Now turn left along its pavement and follow it under a railway bridge and the A41 bridge, then cross the A4251 again and joining the Chiltern Way, take fenced path HH99 bearing left along the foot of the A41 embankment. By a pedestrian tunnel bear half right passing between bollards and through a kissing-gate frame, then take a hedged path (still HH99) uphill to a kissing-gate. Go through this, then fork right onto path HH100 climbing through woodland and soon joining a track. Some 15 yards beyond a right-hand bend, fork left onto a path through the woods. On reaching another flinty track (byway HH101), turn right onto it, soon reaching Felden Lane, then turn left onto this road and follow it uphill into Felden.

Where the road bears left by the entrance to Roefields Close, fork half right onto path HH105, a macadam drive leading to Felden Lodge, and follow this through a wood and out onto a golf course. Halfway across the golf course, leave the drive and bear half left to reach a kissing-gate. Go through this and a second kissing-gate then bear half right across a field to pass through a third kissing-gate by a garage right of a house and bungalow. Here cross a drive and follow a left-hand hedge to cross a stile into a field, then follow a right-hand hedge straight on to a squeeze-stile into Longcroft Lane.

Turn right onto this road and follow it past a large house called Felden Barns to a sharp left-hand bend. Here leave the road and take path HH112 straight on over a stile and across a field to a hedge gap at the far side of the field. Now on path BV16, bear half right across a second field to join the edge of Bury Wood by a clump of trees in the field concealing a pond. Bear slightly left here and follow the outside edge of the wood, later a right-hand hedge, straight on to a stile into a fenced path leading to a second stile. Now turn right and follow the right-hand hedge around a field corner and then straight on along the edge of a prairie field for over half a mile to cross a stile at the far end of the field. Here, leaving the Chiltern Way, bear half right onto path BV17 across a field towards Bovingdon Church to a stile, then continue straight on to a stile. Cross this and a further stile to reach Church Street, Bovingdon opposite the church.

Set in one of the largest churchyards in Hertfordshire, Bovingdon Church was rebuilt in 1845 on the site of a thirteenth-century predecessor, from which the effigy of a knight dating from around 1400 is preserved. The village to your left has some attractive old cottages, but has been rather swamped by modern development.

Fork right onto the road passing the church, then at a sharp left-hand bend, turn right onto byway BV20, a rough lane called Stoney Lane, following it straight on for half a mile until you reach a number of houses. By a right-hand house with lattice windows called Huntsmoor, turn left onto a macadam residential road and follow it out to the B4505.

Turn right onto this road, passing a brick-and-flint lodge to your left. Just past this lodge, cross the road and take a macadam drive opposite (path BV23), turning immediately right over a stile by a gate. Now follow the obvious path straight on through Gorsefield Wood, eventually emerging onto a macadam golf club road. Turn right onto this road following it past the car park and the clubhouse, then bearing left to reach some former farm buildings. By these buildings, the road turns right and where it ends, keep left of a hedge and follow it straight on, then continue along a grassy track (still path BV23) with fine views ahead across the Bulbourne valley with Berkhamsted to your left and the edge of Hemel Hempstead to your right. Having passed two bungalows, where the track ends, go straight on past a rustic seat, then by a small protruding oak tree, turn left, passing just right of a clump of trees with the fourteenth green to your right. Also to your right is an imposing early nineteenth-century manor house called Westbrook Hay which, at one time, housed the offices of the Hemel Hempstead New Town Development Corporation. Now continue straight on downhill passing right of the thirteenth green then bearing slightly left to cross a bridge over the A41. At the far end of the bridge take fenced bridleway HH115 wending its way downhill to a gate and stile into a green lane. Here take the green lane straight on to the A4251 at Bourne End.

Cross this road and turn right onto its pavement. After some 350 yards, just before a petrol station, turn left down a narrow lane called Winkwell, soon crossing a narrow bridge over the River Bulbourne. On reaching the Winkwell Swing Bridge over the Grand Union Canal, opposite the picturesque sixteenth-century 'Three Horseshoes', turn right onto the canal towpath. Now follow the towpath in its deceptively rural setting frequented by ducks and fishermen, for just over a mile, passing under a railway bridge and later a small road bridge. On reaching a second road bridge by the 'Fishery Inn', climb a shallow flight of steps to Fishery Road, then turn right and almost immediately left, crossing the road and passing through a kissing-gate. Now take macadam path HH98 across Boxmoor Common to a second kissing-gate and a pelican crossing on the A4251 where the railway station is in front of you.

WALK 7:   Berkhamsted (North)

Length of Walk: (A) 7.9 miles / 12.7 Km
                              (B) 2.1 miles / 3.4 Km
                              (C) 5.2 miles / 8.3 Km

Starting Point: (A/B) Road junction by northern entrance
                                 to Berkhamsted Railway Station.
                              (C) Potten End Village Hall.

Grid Ref: (A/B)   SP994082
                                (C)   TL016089

Maps: OS Landranger Sheets 165 (A/B only) & 166 (all)
         OS Explorer Sheets 181 (A/B only) & 182 (A/C only)
         OS Pathfinder Sheets 1095 (TL01/11) (A/C only) &
         1118 (SP80/90) (or old Explorer Sheet 2) (A/B only) &
         1119 (TL00/10) (all)
         Chiltern Society FP Map No. 20 (all) or No. 17 (B only).

How to get there / Parking: (A/B) From the junction of the
         old A4251 and A416 in Berkhamsted town centre, take the
         Potten End road and park either in the car park on the
         left or at the railway station.
         (C) Potten End. 1.8 miles northeast of Berkhamsted, may
         be reached from the town by taking one of several
         signposted routes. On reaching the village green, ignore
         two turnings to the right and park in a small car park on
         your right opposite the village hall.

Notes: Heavy nettle growth may be encountered in summer
         particularly on path GG68 on Walks A and C.

Berkhamsted, with its centre in the bottom of a steep-sided river valley, is, in many ways, a typical Chiltern town as it has spread first along its valley and later up the hills on either side. Nevertheless its history sets it apart from its neighbours. In 1066, William the Conqueror, following his victory at the Battle of Hastings, passed through the town on his circuitous approach to London and here accepted the surrender of the Saxon nobles. Shortly after this, he gave the manor to his half-brother, Robert of Mortain who built a castle in this strategically important defile through the Chilterns as a way of protecting London from possible attack. This castle was later destroyed and was rebuilt by the famous Archbishop of

WALK 7

42

Canterbury, Thomas à Becket. The ruins of this castle, which was last occupied in 1496, can still be seen today near the railway station. Amongst the prominent names linked with the castle are the Black Prince who lived in it as Duke of Cornwall, King John of France who was imprisoned there in 1361 and the poet, Geoffrey Chaucer who was at one time its Clerk of Works. Another poet associated with the town is William Cowper, born the son of its rector in 1731, and monuments both to him and his mother are to be found in the thirteenth-century parish church, one of the largest in Hertfordshire.

Walks A and B lead you from the town to its extensive heathy and wooded common returning with fine views over the town, while Walks A and C explore the quiet ridges and valleys beyond with their small picturesque villages and scenic views.

Starting from the road junction by the northern entrance to Berkhamsted railway station, **Walks A and B** take Brownlow Road northwards past the ruins of Berkhamsted Castle. At a right-hand bend, fork left onto Castle Hill and follow this road straight on uphill. At a left-hand bend by the entrance to Berkhamsted Cricket Club, leave the road and take path BK1 straight on over a stile into the Wellcome Foundation car park, then follow a private road straight on to a second car park. Now take a grassy track straight on beside a powerline to a gate and stile, then follow a left-hand fence straight on to a pair of stiles at the far side of the field. Cross the right-hand stile and follow a left-hand hedge straight on through three fields to a stile leading to a track junction at Well Farm. Here turn right onto the right-hand track (path NC58), passing right of the farm buildings, then climbing to join a macadam drive by a bungalow. Where this drive bears right, leave it and go straight on over a stile onto Berkhamsted Common. Now take the obvious scrubland path NC56 straight on.

After 50 yards **Walk B** turns right onto bridleway NC57, soon reaching New Road. Cross this, bearing slightly right and continue uphill (still on bridleway NC57). At a fork bear left and on emerging onto a golf course, go straight on to the left-hand side of a clump of bushes, then bear right through the bushes to reach a rough road. Turn right onto this road rejoining Walk A then read the last paragraph. **Walk A** takes bridleway NC56 straight on. On reaching a track near New Road to your right, take a permissive bridleway straight on to a rough car park. Now continue to a road junction near a war memorial. Here cross the major road and take bridleway NP23 straight on, passing right of the war memorial and crossing a golf fairway. In the next tree belt, look out for a signposted fork to the left. Fork left onto this defined path and follow it straight on across a fairway, through a tree belt and across another fairway to reach waymarked path NP18 between garden hedges.

Walks A and C follow this path to cross a residential road, then take a fenced path straight on. On entering Great Frithsden Copse, disregard a crossing path and go straight on for some 400 yards. Where another path merges from your right, bear slightly left and continue downhill to a road at the scattered hamlet of Frithsden (pronounced 'Freezeden').

Turn right onto this road passing two houses, then after about 80 yards turn left over a stile in a wall under a tree onto fenced path NP19 and follow it to a stile. Cross this and follow a right-hand hedge uphill. On reaching a barbed-wire fence near Highridge Farm, cross a stile a few yards to your right and follow a fenced path past the farm to a stile leading to a stony track on the ridgetop, where Ashridge House, rebuilt for the seventh Earl of Bridgewater by Wyatt in the early nineteenth century, comes into view on a hill to your left. Turn right onto this track and follow it through two fields. On reaching double gates, turn left to cross a further stile leading to a rough road known locally as 'Roman Road'.

Now ignore a stile to your left and turn left onto the rough road. Where it starts to descend into a walled cutting constructed for the canal-building third Duke of Bridgewater, fork right through a squeeze-stile by a gate onto path NP8 turning left over a stile into a belt of trees. Now follow this path downhill through the tree belt beside the sunken way, passing through a squeeze-stile by an old bridge over the sunken way and continuing downhill to reach a flight of steps descending to rejoin the road. Now follow this downhill into Nettleden, a tiny village with picturesque seventeenth-century cottages and a church rebuilt in brick in 1811 but retaining its fifteenth-century tower.

At a T-junction, turn left onto a road passing double gates, then turn right through an anti-horse barrier onto path NP9 uphill between hedges past two fields. Now cross a stile and take path GG76 following a right-hand hedge through a field containing Buddhist shrines. At the far side of this field, continue along a fenced path which joins a gravel drive and leads to a road at St. Margaret's, named after the former twelfth-century nunnery of St. Margaret de Bosco.

Turn left onto this road, then, after about 50 yards, turn right over a concealed stile by a gate onto path GG78. Now bear slightly left, following the outside edge of St. Margaret's Copse downhill to a stile. Here leave the wood and go straight on across a field, passing right of a clump of hawthorn bushes, then bearing slightly left to reach a stile by a twin-poled electricity pylon. Cross this and take path GG1, bearing half right across a field to a stile and kissing-gate right of a long line of concrete garages at Great Gaddesden. Here bear half right onto path GG2 passing through a kissing-gate and following the churchyard wall beneath a row of lime trees. At the far end of the churchyard, turn left over a stile into it and follow a right-hand wall through the churchyard to a lychgate.

Great Gaddesden's twelfth-century church with its massive fifteenth-century tower decorated with gargoyles is notable for the Roman bricks used in its construction, which are believed to have derived from a Roman villa on the same site, and the early Georgian Halsey mausoleum containing more than twenty monuments.

Now go through the lychgate and take a road, bearing right and ignoring a turning to the left. At a T-junction by the 'Cock and Bottle', turn right, then immediately left onto fenced path GG68 leading to a stile.Now continue between hedges to cross a further stile, then follow a left-hand hedge straight on across a field to a stile at its far end. Cross this, then turn right over a second stile onto fenced path GG67, following it uphill into Highpark Wood. Just inside the wood, turn left onto path GG69 and follow it along the inside edge of the wood for nearly half a mile with views to your left at first across Water End in the Gade valley towards Gaddesden Place on the hill opposite, built by Wyatt for the Halseys in 1768–1773 and still their home today. On reaching a T-junction of paths, turn left onto path GG67, soon crossing a stile into a field with a view across the valley towards Potten End on the next ridge. Now go straight on downhill heading for the corner of a hedge on the hillside opposite to reach a stile onto Nettleden Road.

Cross this road and a stile opposite, then go straight on, now heading for the near corner of a wood called Brown's Spring and ignoring a branching path to your left (where you join path NP7) to reach a marker post. Now turn left onto path NP31 to the corner of a hedge where you turn right and follow the nearside of the hedge to a stile in a corner of the field, then go straight on, entering the wood and following its inside edge to a stile. Cross this and follow an enclosed path uphill ignoring a branching path to your right, soon passing gardens and going through a kissing-gate and eventually reaching Water End Road on the edge of Potten End. Turn right onto its pavement and follow the major road straight on for half a mile, ignoring all side turnings, to reach the village hall.

From Potten End village hall, where **Walk C** starts, **Walks A and C** follow the Berkhamsted road to the edge of the village green, then opposite the turning to Bourne End, turn right onto bridleway NP22 following a gravel drive towards a house called 'Bryher'.

About 25 yards short of its gate, turn left onto a path following the inside edge of the wood and ignoring all branching and crossing paths. On reaching a sunken gully, part of the ancient earthwork known as Grim's Ditch, enter it and follow it straight on for a quarter mile, crossing a golf course at one point, to reach Nettleden Road. Turn right onto this road, then almost immediately left. Now **Walk C** takes the right-hand of two bridleways (NP24) straight on, ignoring all lesser branching paths. On emerging onto the golf course, bear slightly left, following an obvious path passing left of the 16th tee and right of the 15th green and heading towards a prominent birch tree on the edge of the wood ahead. Just before reaching this tree, turn right onto waymarked path NP18 between garden hedges. Now go back to the top of page 44.

Now go back to the top of page 44.

Walk A takes the left-hand of the two bridleways (NP23) and follows its winding course through woodland, ignoring lesser branching paths and soon reaching a fairway. Go straight on across this into further woodland. Here keep right at a fork, then go straight on, crossing two further fairways to pass left of the war memorial and reach a road junction where you turn left onto the Potten End and Water End road. Now follow this road to the entrance to Berkhamsted Golf Club, then turn right onto it. Where the macadam road turns left, leave it and take a rough road straight on.

At the end of the road by the gate of 'Fairhill', **Walks A and B** bear half right onto path BK2 into woodland, keeping left at a fork and following a garden wall to a stile. Cross this and a second stile with a superb view across Berkhamsted beginning to open out ahead, then follow a left-hand fence to a stile by a cattle grid. Now take a concrete road to cross another stile by a cattle grid, then follow the left-hand hedge generally straight on through three fields. At the far end of the third field, turn right and follow a left-hand hedge, later a line of beech trees downhill to a stile onto New Road opposite the ruins of Berkhamsted Castle. Cross the road, then turn left onto its pavement and follow it to a crossroads. Here fork right into a road called White Hill and follow it beside the railway back to Berkhamsted Station.

WALK 8: Berkhamsted (South)

Length of Walk:	8.3 miles / 13.3 Km
Starting Point:	Junction of A4251 (High Street) and A416 (Kings Road), Berkhamsted.
Grid Ref:	SP991079

Maps: OS Landranger Sheet 165
OS Explorer Sheet 181 (or old Sheet 2)
OS Pathfinder Sheet 1118 (SP80/90)
Chiltern Society FP Maps Nos. 8 & 17

Parking: There are several public car parks in the centre of Berkhamsted.

Notes: Heavy nettle growth may be found in summer on bridleway AG2 and path BK46.

Berkhamsted, the name of which is locally pronounced 'Berk'msted' and has, till quite recently, been prone to a number of variations in spelling, is described in the introduction to Walk 7.

The walk takes you westwards uphill through leafy suburbs to cross the bypass and continue by way of the lost village of Marlin to the hilltop Buckinghamshire village of Hawridge with its moated manor house. From here, it takes you south-eastwards along the crest of a ridge and then down into Chesham Vale before returning by way of Ashley Green and Hockeridge Wood to Berkhamsted.

Starting from the junction of the old A4251 (High Street) and the A416 (Kings Road), take Kings Road uphill. After some 200 yards, turn right into Charles Street, then take the second turning left, Doctors Commons Road. Opposite No. 19, turn right into a fenced alleyway (path BK14). Follow this straight on, joining a right-hand road for a few yards and then leaving it again, crossing a drive and eventually emerging into North Road. Turn left into this road, then immediately right into Anglefield Road and after about 25 yards, fork left onto path BK15, an alleyway left of a double garage and follow it straight on to reach a narrow lane without pavements. Turn left into this lane and ignore first a left-hand turn, then a right-hand turn called Greystoke Close. Opposite a house called 'Chilterns', turn right onto path BK18, a fenced alleyway by the entrance to 'Little Corner'

WALK 8

BERKHAMSTED

ASHLEY GREEN

CHESHAM VALE

HAWRIDGE

HEATH END

48

and follow it straight on, crossing another alley and two roads and eventually emerging onto a third road at the edge of the town.

Turn right onto this road, then immediately left through gates into a rough lane (bridleway BK33) and follow it downhill. At the bottom, on entering a field, follow a left-hand hedge straight on to a stile in the bypass fence. Cross this stile and turn right to descend a flight of steps then cross the A41 via a gap in its central reservation crash-barrier and climb another flight of steps to a stile. Here join bridleway NC21 following a rough track straight on beside a left-hand hedge. Where the track passes through a hedge gap into another field, continue to follow it straight on, now with a hedge to your right. Near the far end of this field, follow the track reverting to the other side of the hedge. Now take bridleway NC20, a wide grassy lane, straight on, keeping left of a wood called Cock Grove and passing Marlin Chapel Farm, where there are traces of a moat and it would appear that there might once have been a village.

Where the lane opens out into a field, leave the track, bearing slightly right and passing right of the ruins of St. Mary Magdalene's Chapel (already a ruin in 1822) to a gate and stile into Rossway Park with a view of Rossway House ahead. Now go straight on across the park, gradually diverging from a left-hand fence to reach a stile left of a bungalow on the far side of the park. Cross this stile and a rough lane and take path WG4 straight on through a hedge gap, following a right-hand hedge downhill to a stile in the valley bottom. Cross this and turn right onto a road following the Buckinghamshire boundary; then at a fork, bear left onto the road signposted to Wigginton and Tring. Just past a right-hand copse, turn left through a gap in the roadside bank onto bridleway CY36, following the left-hand side of a strip of grass, later a hedge uphill to reach an iron gate. Do not go through this gate, but instead turn left onto path CY38 and follow a right-hand hedge, soon passing a plantation to reach a stile. Cross this stile, then turn left and follow a left-hand hedge to a field corner. Here turn right and continue to follow the left-hand hedge through two fields to a stile into a rough lane near Hill Farm.

Turn right into the lane and follow it downhill, bearing right at the bottom to reach a road junction by Vale Farm on the edge of Hawridge Common. Turn sharp left onto the road, then immediately fork right opposite a rusty white gate onto path CY48, climbing across the wooded common to emerge onto a road at the top of the hill opposite Church Lane. Cross this road and take Church Lane straight on to reach Hawridge Church with its green-painted bellcote, built in 1856 on the site of its thirteenth-century predecessor, and Hawridge Court, a timber-framed manor house with a partially filled moat.

By the entrance to Hawridge Court, turn right onto path CY39, a narrow alleyway between a hedge and a cottage, to reach a stile into a field where the moat is visible to your left. In the field, turn left onto path CY31, briefly joining Bucks Walk 6. Now cross a stile by a gate in the corner of the field and go straight on across the next field to a stile at the far side. Cross this and follow a grassy track straight on along the crest of the ridge through two large fields with fine views of Hawridge Vale to your left, a Victorian house called Thorne Barton on a hilltop near Ashley Green ahead and the outskirts of Chesham further to the right. After nearly three-quarters of a mile, at the far end of the second field, go through a hedge gap then turn left and follow the left-hand hedge downhill to a corner of the field. Here turn right and continue to follow a left-hand hedge to the bottom corner of the field. Now turn left over a stile onto path CY54, a grassy hedged lane, and follow it straight on for over 300 yards, with the right-hand hedge later giving way to a fence, to reach a gate and stile leading to the road in Chesham Vale.

Turn left onto this road joining Bucks Walk 7. Opposite the 'Black Horse' turn right onto bridleway CY51 (later AG1c), a rough sunken lane, and follow it straight on for a quarter mile. Where the lane forks and the left-hand option goes straight on to a gate into a wood, turn right onto bridleway AG2; then, where the main track turns right again through large green gates, leave it and take a narrower sunken track straight on, climbing gradually through a copse and past a pond. At the top of the hill, follow the lane bearing left and continuing between hedges for some 300 yards until you reach the end of a concrete farm road. Go straight on along this, swinging right to reach Flamstead Farm. Here turn left (still on AG2) and leaving Bucks Walk 7, pass left of a Dutch barn to a gate into another hedged lane, which you follow for a quarter mile to reach a road called Hog Lane on the edge of Ashley Green.

Cross this road and take fenced path AG2e straight on to a stile into a field, then follow a left-hand hedge straight on to the corner of the field. Here transfer through a gap in the left-hand hedge to its other side and follow it downhill, turning left then right at one point, to reach a stile into Hockeridge Wood. Having crossed this, ignore a crossing path and take a woodland track straight on for a third of a mile, disregarding a crossing track by a picnic table. On passing a small picnic area to your right with three tables, turn right onto path AG17a, a flinty track and follow this downhill, ignoring three right-hand forking tracks, to reach a crossing track at the bottom marking the county boundary. Cross this and take path BK46 straight on uphill. Near a right-hand bungalow, where the path turns left, leave it bearing right to cross a stile out of the wood. Now follow the outside edge of the wood straight on to a corner of the wood, then bear half right across the field to white gates leading to the A416.

50

Turn left onto this road and follow it to a new roundabout. Here take the A416 straight on to cross a bridge over the bypass. At the far end of the bridge, turn left over a stile onto path BK44 and follow it through woodland known as Brickhill Green. At the far side of the wood, turn right onto path BK45 and follow it along the inside edge of the wood to the A416. Cross this main road bearing slightly left and take path BK13 through a fence gap with an old kissing-gate frame. Now follow a line of trees straight on across a school playing field with views across Berkhamsted to the hills beyond. At the far side, take an alleyway straight on downhill, soon passing a field to your right, to reach another school playing field. Go straight on along the edge of this playing field then take an alleyway left of a school (path BK9) straight on, soon turning right to reach the end of a cul-de-sac street. Turn left to reach the High Street, then left again for your starting point.

WALK 9: Northchurch Common

Length of Walk: 6.9 miles / 11.2 Km

Starting Point: Informal car park at bend in B4506 half a mile north of Northchurch.

Grid Ref: SP979095

Maps: OS Landranger Sheet 165
OS Explorer Sheet 181 (or old Sheet 2)
OS Pathfinder Sheets 1094 (SP81/91) & 1118 (SP80/90)
Chiltern Society FP Maps Nos. 17 & 19

How to get there / Parking: Northchurch Common, 1.5 miles northwest of Berkhamsted, may be reached from the town by taking the A4251 northwestwards to Northchurch, then turning right onto the B4506 and following it for half a mile to a sharp left-hand bend. Here ignore a turning to the right, then almost immediately turn right into a grassy car park.

Northchurch Common on the hill above Northchurch is one of a belt of largely wooded commons stretching from the outskirts of Berkhamsted to Aldbury and Ivinghoe Beacon now managed by the National Trust. The village in the Bulbourne valley below, which you skirt early in the walk, is today little more than a suburb of nearby Berkhamsted, but it was once more important than its urban neighbour. In Roman times Northchurch was the site of a small town and in Saxon times it had a castle and a stone-built church, part of which is incorporated in the present largely thirteenth-century building. In the church is a brass memorial to Peter the Wildboy who became famous in 1725 after being found living wild in the woods near Hamelin in King George I's country of birth and joint kingdom, the Electorate of Hanover. Peter was brought to England by the King, but, when it proved impossible to educate him, he was sent to a farm in Northchurch where he spent the rest of his left and was buried in 1785. In more modern times, although the relative importance of Northchurch has declined, its location on various major transport routes through the Chilterns has caused it to grow and develop into a commuter dormitory.

The walks first leads you down towards Northchurch to join the Grand Union Canal towpath and follow it for over a mile to Cow Roast Lock. Having left the canal, you walk over a hill to the picturesque village of Aldbury before climbing the wooded escarpment to reach the Bridgewater Monument. From here the walk returns by way of Aldbury's wooden common, with a fine view of Tring and the Vale of Aylesbury, and Northchurch Common with its mixture of open grassland and heathland to your starting point.

Starting from the entrance to the car park, turn left onto the B4506 and follow it downhill towards Northchurch for nearly half a mile to the bridge over the Grand Union Canal on the edge of the village. Having crossed this bridge, turn right through a gap by a gate onto the canal towpath at Northchurch Lock. Follow this pleasant waterside path northwestwards for three-quarters of a mile to a road bridge at Dudswell. Turn right over this bridge, then immediately left rejoining the towpath at Dudswell Lock and following it for over half a mile to bridge no. 137 at Cow Roast Lock, the name of which is thought to be a corruption of 'Cow Rest' as the nearby 'Cow Roast Inn' may have been a resting place for cattle drovers on their way down the modern A4251 to the London markets.

Pass under the bridge, climb a flight of steps to the lock, then turn sharp right between walls to reach Wharf Lane. Joining the Chiltern Way, turn left onto this road and follow it for about 150 yards, then turn left over a stile onto path NC29 and go straight across a field to an ungainly footbridge over the railway. Having crossed this bridge, keep straight on across the next field to a gap in a fenced hedge. Go through this gap then turn right onto a fenced farm track, soon turning left and crossing a stile by a gate by the farmhouse at Norcott Court Farm.

On reaching the farm drive, turn left onto it then cross a stile by a gate and turn right, keeping right of farm buildings to cross a stile by a gate. Still on NC29 bear half left, crossing the field diagonally with fine views across the Bulbourne valley to your left and behind you, to cross a stile by a gate in the far corner. Here take a grassy track to the corner of a right-hand tree belt then bear slightly left across the field to the corner of a hedge. Follow this hedge straight on to a corner of the field then turn right through a hedge gap and belt of trees to a stile. Here take path AB3 bearing half left across a field to a stile in the top left-hand corner where a fine view opens out through the Tring Gap towards the Aylesbury Vale beyond. Cross this stile and follow the edge of a right-hand wood called The Hangings straight on, ignoring a crossing bridleway (where you leave the Chiltern Way).

At the corner of the wood turn right, following the edge of the wood for a further 200 yards, with a fine view ahead of Aldbury hidden in trees backed by Clipper Down, then cross a stile by a gate into a hedged lane and follow it along the edge of the wood. On emerging into a field, bear half left across it, heading for the left-hand corner of a copse, with the top of the Bridgewater Monument visible over the treetops to your right, to cross two stiles, then bear slightly left to a third stile leading onto Newground Road.

Turn left onto this road, then at a left-hand bend, just before a concrete drive, turn right through a hedge gap onto path AB68 and bear half right across a field to the far corner of the field. Here go through a handgate and bear half right again, following the right-hand hedge to cross a stile at the far end of the field. Now follow a left-hand hedge straight on to cross a further stile into a hedged path. Take this path to reach the end of a village street in Aldbury, then follow this street straight on past the 'Valiant Trooper' to the picturesque village green with its pond, ancient stocks, seventeenth-century manor house and a number of attractive cottages.

Joining the reverse direction of Walk 12 take Stocks Road straight on past the green and the 'Greyhound' and out of the village. Some 200 yards beyond its last cottage, having rounded a left-hand bend, turn right onto path AB33 up some steps, through a hedge gap and over a stile and follow a left-hand hedge uphill for some 50 yards until you reach a stile in it. Cross this then (leaving Walk 12 again) take path AB32 bearing half right across a field to a stile into a wood some distance to the right of an imposing house on the hillside called Little Stocks. Inside the wood take a path straight on, ignoring two crossing paths and climbing steeply to reach a T-junction of paths near a cottage. Here turn right onto bridleway AB29 keeping right at a fork and soon entering a small clearing. At the far side of the clearing bear slightly left, disregarding a crossing bridleway and continuing through beechwoods to emerge in a clearing by the Bridgewater Monument, erected in 1832 in memory of the third Duke of Bridgewater (1736–1803), 'the Father of the English canal system'. This monument stands at the end of a 1.5-mile-long avenue known as Prince's Riding which was laid out in about 1760 as part of Ashridge Park and the house, rebuilt by James Wyatt and Sir Jeffry Wyatville between 1803 and 1820, can just be seen at the other end.

By the monument turn right along the edge of the clearing to join a stony track (bridleway AB20). Bear slightly right onto this, re-entering the woods, ignoring a lesser fork to the left and passing through a clearing planted with young trees with a fine view ahead across Aldbury towards Tring. On entering mature woodland, ignore a branching bridleway to the right and a crossing path, then at a fork go

WALK 9

Little Stocks
AB 29
AB 32
Stock's Farm
Walk 12
AB 33
AB 20
AB 20
AB 26
CP
AB 21
'Greyhound'
Walk 12
ALDBURY
AB 11a
'Valiant Trooper'
AB 68
Newground Road
AB 68
AB 3
The Hangings
Chiltern Way
AB 3
NC 29
Norcott Court Farm
NC 29
Cow Roast Lock
NC 29
Chiltern Way
'Cow Roast Inn'
A4251
Wharf Lane
Grand Union
Dudswell Lock
Canal
DUDSWELL
N
A4251
'Old Grey Mare'
B4506
TUNNEL
NORTHCHURCH
'George & Dragon'

Bridgewater Monument
B4506
Prince's
Riding
Ashridge
AB 20
AB 12
Walk 13
AB 21
Walk 13
Aldbury
Common
AB 11a
AB 11a
Aldbury
Common
AB 11a
NC 32
NC 32
NC 34
Northchurch
NC 34
Common
NC 34
Northchurch Farm
NC 34
CP Start

0 _____ 1 mile
0 _____ 1 kilometre

55

right onto bridleway AB26, a sunken track dropping through beechwoods towards Aldbury. After about 100 yards join bridleway AB21 which merges from your left, then after a further 140 yards, at a path junction with a steep chalk face to your left, bear half left onto bridleway AB11a, a gently rising sunken path which soon enters an ancient yew wood, now with a fence to your right. Where a path commences on top of the right-hand bank of the gully, take this path, keeping parallel to the gully and ignoring a crossing path. Eventually this path leads you to a clearing with a bench. At the far end of the clearing, crossing the Chiltern Way, bear half left onto the right-hand of two bridleways (still AB11a) entering mature woodland. On reaching a rough drive, continue straight across it and ignore all other crossing tracks until you reach the macadam road across Aldbury Common.

Cross this road and take well-used bridleway AB11a straight on for a quarter mile ignoring all crossing paths until a field comes into view to your right. Now go straight on for a further quarter mile, after 250 yards keeping left at a fork to reach a fork by a corner of the right-hand field. Here keep left then at a second fork go right onto bridleway NC32 which soon bears left into an area of bracken on Northchurch Common. Soon the bracken to your left gives way to open grassland and Berkhamsted comes into view ahead. On reaching another area of wooded common, ignore crossing tracks and go straight on into the wooded area. At a six-way junction by the corner of more grassland bear half left onto bridleway NC34 and follow it straight on along the edge of this grassland for over a third of a mile, passing through a dip where Northchurch can be seen to your right and reaching another rise. About 100 yards before the far end of the grassland, by a group of young silver birch trees, turn right onto a mown grassy track through the bracken (still NC34) and follow it downhill ignoring all crossing tracks. After crossing a flint track, you start climbing again and soon reach the B4506. Cross this road and take bridleway NC34 straight on over the top of a hill, ignoring a branching bridleway to your left and descending to reach scrubland. Where the mown path turns left, leave it and take a narrower path straight on into the bushes, crossing a macadam drive and eventually reaching the grassy clearing by the B4506 at your starting point.

WALK 10:   Tring

Length of Walk: 6.8 miles / 11.0 Km
Starting Point: 'Rose and Crown Hotel', Tring.
Grid Ref: SP925114
Maps: OS Landranger Sheet 165
           OS Explorer Sheet 181 (or old Sheet 2)
           OS Pathfinder Sheets 1094 (SP81/91) & 1118 (SP80/90)
           Chiltern Society FP Map No. 18
Parking: Public car park on the north side of Tring High
    Street just east of Tring Church.
Notes: Heavy nettle growth may be encountered in places in
    summer months.

Tring, situated at a gap in the Chiltern escarpment, has always been a place of some importance as it straddles Akeman Street, a Roman road from London to Cirencester, near its junction with the Ancient British Upper Icknield Way which itself passes through the suburbs of the town. In more modern times Tring has also found itself on the routes of various generations of main traffic arteries in the form of the A41 trunk road from London to Aylesbury and Birmingham, the Grand Union Canal from London to the Midlands and the London Midland main railway from Euston to Birmingham and the North. The town boasts a principally fifteenth-century church with a Grinling Gibbons monument to Sir William Gore dating from 1707. Not far from the town centre is a large mansion called Tring Park which was originally designed by Sir Christopher Wren. This house, reputedly often visited in its early years by Nell Gwynne, was for two centuries the home of the family of Sir William Gore, the first Director of the Bank of England. It was later acquired by the Rothschilds who enlarged the house giving it its Victorian appearance. The surrounding park, once noted for its tranquillity, was desecrated in the 1970s by the building of the Tring Bypass which severs the house from the bulk of the park, but if one can ignore the traffic, it remains a place of beauty.

    The walk takes you from Tring through Tring Park and across the bypass, then climbs the wooded escarpment to reach

WALK 10

N

Start

TRING

B 486

'Bell' CP

'Rose &Crown'
TU 37

The Mansion

B 4635

A 4251

B 4635

'Castle'

Tring Park

A 41

TU 19

Hastoe Lane

TU 21

Obelisk

TU 22 TU 22 TU 21

Ridgeway Path

A 41

TU 30 TU 26

West Leith Farm

Stubbings Wood

Tring Park

Park Wood

TU 80

Bucks Walk 3

TU 31

TU 28

TU 75

DB 31

TU 34 TU 31

TU 36

TU 80

Greyhound

TERRIER'S END

TU 18

WIGGINTON

HANG HILL

DB 24

B 20

DB 25

Wick Farm

DB 22

B 19

HASTOE

B 22

Painsend Farm

Hastoe Cross

TU 18

Wick Wood

Pavis Wood

TU 14

Chiltern Way

DB 28

DB 27

Shire Lane

Brown's Lane

Grim's Ditch

High Scrubs

B 22

Ridgeway Path

DB 29

DB 27

B 25

TU 17

TU 14

Chiltern Way

Northill Wood

B 24

Bucks Walk 3

TU 16

Longcroft

CY 7

Grim's Ditch

CY 7

B 25

0 ———————————————— 1mile

0 ———————————————— 1kilometre

58

the edge of Wigginton. It then skirts the village and continues towards Hastoe, then later follows an ancient earthwork known as Grim's Ditch across the plateau into Buckinghamshire before descending through beechwoods to the isolated hamlet of Hang Hill and returning to Tring.

Starting from the 'Rose and Crown Hotel' opposite Tring Church, take the High Street westwards for about 50 yards. Just before a zebra crossing, turn left into a narrow alleyway (path TU37). At a T-junction of paths, turn left, soon turning right again to resume your previous direction, then go straight on to reach Park Street opposite one of the lodges of Tring Park. Cross this road bearing slightly right and take fenced macadam path TU19 to a spiralled footbridge over the A41 into Tring Park. At the far end of the bridge, go through a kissing-gate onto fenced path TU21 following the bypass fence straight on, then after a few yards, bearing half right across the outer part of the park, with views over your left shoulder of Tring Park House. On crossing a stile by a gate to enter Park Wood, follow a flint track (path TU22) uphill through the woods to an obelisk. Legend has it that this obelisk was erected by Charles II in memory of Nell Gwynne, but as he died first, this seems unlikely.

Just before the obelisk, turn right, crossing another track and taking a narrower path (still TU22) steeply uphill. At the top at a junction of tracks and paths, bear half left onto path TU21, a track alongside a plantation, soon reaching a gate and gap by a house. Go through the gap, then turn right over a stile onto path TU80. Now follow a left-hand hedge straight on along the edge of the plantation, ignoring branching paths to the right and garden entrances to the left and at one point passing through a squeeze-stile. On reaching a crossing macadam drive, go straight on between gardens, later turning right and eventually reaching a stile, then turn left onto a fenced path leading to a stile at the far end of the adjoining field into a stony lane near the end of a village street at Wigginton.

Turn right into this lane (path TU18) and follow it across the upland plateau for over three-quarters of a mile, passing Wick Farm and eventually reaching a macadam road near a road junction at Hastoe, the highest village in Hertfordshire. Turn left onto this road and follow it for a quarter mile. Where a left-hand wood ends and a right-hand wood called High Scrubs begins, joining the Chiltern Way, turn right over a stile into High Scrubs and bear slightly right onto TU14, the right-hand of two woodland paths. This path follows Grim's Ditch, an ancient earthwork of unknown origin clearly visible to your right, straight on through the wood for a quarter mile, then goes straight across a field to a hedge gap ahead. Here cross a rough lane called Brown's Lane and go straight on through another hedge gap. Now follow the left side of a belt of trees concealing Grim's Ditch to the far end of the field. Here, leaving the Chiltern Way, turn right onto path TU16 through the tree belt crossing Grim's Ditch. On entering another field, go straight on for a few yards to the beginning of another tree belt, then turn left through a hedge gap onto path TU17 following a left-hand hedge to a stile and gate onto a road called Shire Lane which forms the boundary between Hertfordshire and Buckinghamshire.

Turn left onto this road and after some 60 yards, opposite Longcroft farmhouse, turn right onto bridleway CY7, a macadam farm road. Take this straight on for a third of a mile passing a few houses and some farm buildings in a hollow. At the top of the next rise, turn right over a stile opposite a handgate onto path B25 and go straight across a large arable field to enter the distant Pavis Wood near where a hedge to the right reaches it. Inside the wood take path DB27 generally straight on, soon crossing the heavily-used Ridgeway Path and following a defined path downhill through a plantation. On entering mature woodland, the path joins a sunken gully and follows it downhill through the wood to the valley bottom.

At the bottom of the hill, by a Buckinghamshire County Council noticeboard, turn sharp left onto bridleway DB28 following the inside edge of the wood along the valley bottom. After 250 yards at a fork go straight on, then, at a T-junction in a corner of the wood, turn right onto hedged path B22. Take this path straight on for a quarter mile. Where it starts to swing perceptibly to the left and a house becomes visible through the trees ahead, turn right onto path B19 passing through a hedge gap into a field. Now follow the left-hand field edge straight on to the far end of the field. Here turn sharp right onto path B20, crossing the field diagonally to a gap between the corner of a fence and the end of a hedge. Go though this gap and take path DB22 following the left-hand fence past some attractive thatched cottages to cross a stile in the corner of the field, then descend through a hedge gap into a narrow road at Hang Hill.

Turn left along this road passing the thatched cottages. Opposite Hang Hill Cottage, turn right through a gate onto path DB25 following a right-hand hedge to the far end of the field. Here take path DB24 straight on, crossing a stile and passing through a hedge gap. Now turn right and follow the right-hand hedge around the bottom of a field past some cottages. Where the hedge turns right, follow it to a hedge gap onto a road at Terrier's End. Turn left onto this road and follow it to a sharp left-hand bend. Here leave the road and take path DB31 through a bridlegate right of a telegraph pole straight on into a field, then go straight on over a rise to a bridlegate right of an ash tree into a hedged lane (byway TU36). Turn left into this lane, re-entering Hertfordshire, then turn immediately right into another hedged lane (byway TU34) which leads you over a rise. Where this lane forks, take the right-hand option and follow this for some 350 yards, swinging right and climbing until you enter Stubbing's Wood. At a T-junction just inside the wood, turn left onto byway TU28, then at a fork, keep right, following the wider track to another T-junction. Here turn left onto byway TU75. Just before a gate at the edge of the wood, turn right onto path TU31, soon passing through a squeeze-stile and following the inside edge of the wood straight on for a third of a mile with views to your left over the Tring Bypass and western part of the town. On nearing the bypass, join path TU30 which merges from your right, then at a T-junction, turn right onto a grassy track uphill into a field. Here bear left following the bypass fence over a slight rise, where there are fine views across Tring towards Ivinghoe Beacon, to reach a gate and stile. Now take path TU26 straight on beside the bypass fence through two more fields to a concrete track descending to a gate and kissing-gate into Hastoe Lane. Cross this road, then turn left along its footway passing under the A41 and continuing to the edge of Tring. At a T-junction turn right then immediately left into Akeman Street following this past the Tring Zoological Museum to reach the High Street. Here turn right for your starting point.

WALK 11:   Marsworth (Startop's End)

Length of Walk: 6.7 miles / 10.8 Km

Starting Point: Entrance to Tring Reservoirs Car Park, Startop's End, Marsworth.

Grid Ref;:   SP919141

Maps: OS Landranger Sheet 165

OS Explorer Sheet 181 (or old Sheet 2)

OS Pathfinder Sheet 1094 (SP81/91)

Chiltern Society FP Map No. 18

How to get there / Parking: Startop's End, 6 miles east of Aylesbury, may be reached from the town by taking the A41 towards Tring to Aston Clinton, then turning left onto the B489 and following it for 2.8 miles to Startop's End. Here just before the 'White Lion' and canal bridge traffic lights, turn right into the Tring Reservoirs Car Park.

Marsworth, with its much-altered twelfth-century church on a prominent hillock at the foot of the Chilterns, is perhaps best known today for the Tring Reservoirs immediately to the south of the village. These were constructed between 1802 and 1839 to supply water to the Grand Junction Canal (since 1929 known as the Grand Union Canal) and today, as well as being popular with anglers, they are frequented by many rare species of water birds and have therefore been designated as a nature reserve. Within the parish are also the junctions of the main Grand Union Canal (constructed between 1793 and 1806) and its Wendover and Aylesbury arms. The latter is noted for its interesting double lock a few yards from the canal junction which takes the canal down into the Vale of Aylesbury. In the half century between the construction of these canals and the coming of the nearby London & North Western main railway line, the canals, which were the brainchild of the third Duke of Bridgewater and his engineer friend, James Brindley, provided the major freight link between London and the industrialised Midlands and North.

The walk, which is of an easy nature, is, indeed, one for the lovers of water as much of it follows the towpaths of the three canals and the banks of the reservoirs, including the beautiful tree-line cutting near Bulbourne. Fine views can also be obtained in places of the nearby escarpment and Vale of Aylesbury.

Starting from the entrance to the Tring Reservoirs car park at Startop's End (pronounced 'Starrups'), take path MW12 walking half the length of the car park then turning right up a flight of steps to reach path MW13 on the banks of Startop's End Reservoir. Turn left onto this and where the path forks by a causeway separating the Startop's End and Marsworth Reservoirs, fork left following path MW14 along the top of the bank until it joins the Grand Union Canal towpath (MW16) at Lock No. 40. Now take this towpath straight on for 1.3 miles, after half a mile crossing a bridge over the mouth of the disused Wendover Arm, then passing the canal workshop and 'Grand Junction Arms' at Bulbourne (pronounced 'Booburn') before going under the B488 (Upper Icknield Way) road bridge to enter the beautiful wooded cutting which marks the highest point of the canal. After a further two-thirds of a mile the path climbs a slope to the Marshcroft Lane bridge where you turn right onto this pleasant, little-used road and follow it for half a mile to its end at Tring Grove on the outskirts of Tring.

Turn right here into Grove Road and follow it for over a third of a mile to a filling station on the left. Now after a further two houses, turn left onto path TU66, an alleyway between the houses, and follow it to the B486. Cross this road and take New Road straight on. On nearing a right-hand bend, just past the Air Training Corps hut, turn right onto macadam path TU78 (signposted to the Icknield Way) and follow it straight on for 200 yards to reach the B488 (Upper Icknield Way). Turn left onto its pavement then having crossed a bridge over a small stream, turn right onto path TU52, a macadam road beside a stream. By a ruined building the road ends and you follow a path beside the stream straight on until it joins the Wendover Arm. Now turn left and follow the bank of this disused canal for nearly half a mile to Little Tring where it becomes dry. Here follow a path straight on through an area of scrub then up a flight of steps to Little Tring Road.

Cross the road and a stile and take path TU67 down a flight of steps, then cross a stile in a left-hand fence and follow the other side of the fence to the far end of the field. Here turn right over three stiles onto path TR46 following a right-hand fence uphill to cross a stile at the top, where there is a fine view of Wilstone Reservoir ahead. Now go straight on downhill to a stile into scrubland. Within the scrubland cross the dry canal, then ignore a stile ahead and turn left onto raised path TR47 and follow this former towpath through scrub. After a quarter mile turn right down some steps and over a stile onto path TR49 which follows a right-hand fence downhill. At a corner of the field turn left and follow a right-hand hedge to the next corner. Here go straight on through a hedge gap, then turn right onto a grassy track following a right-hand hedge. Having passed through another hedge gap, bear half left across the next field to cross a stile at the left-hand edge of a hedge in the far corner. Now take path DB6 following a right-hand stream to a footbridge and stile. Cross these and bear half left across the next field heading towards a stile in the far corner. About 50 yards short of this, turn right onto worn path DB5 crossing the field to cross a stile and footbridge in the far corner. Now ignore a stile to your left and a gate to your right and take fenced path TR44 through a belt of trees. On emerging over a footbridge onto the bank of Wilstone Reservoir, follow this for nearly half a mile to the next corner of the reservoir. Having just rounded this, turn sharp left dropping steeply to the B489 (Lower Icknield Way).

Turn left onto this ancient road, then after some 30 yards turn right over a concealed stile onto path TR33. Now bear half right across a paddock to a stile, then bear slightly left across a second paddock to a stile, footbridge and second stile in the far corner. Cross these and a concrete drive, then go straight on through a handgate and across the corner of a field to a handgate leading to a footbridge and kissing-gate onto a road. Turn right onto this road, then almost immediately left through a kissing-gate and take path TR34 bearing half left across a field to two further kissing-gates at the end of a village street at Wilstone.

Wilstone, which has only had its own church since 1860, is associated with a story of witchcraft, as in 1751 a suspected witch called Ruth Osborn was hounded by the local populace and murdered by a chimneysweep called Colley who allegedly held her head under water in a local pond. While some say these events took place at nearby Long Marston, what is definitely known is that Colley was hanged for it at Hertford Gaol four months later and his body was brought back and hung in chains at nearby Gubblecote as a warning to local people not to take the law into their own hands.

Follow the village street to Wilstone war memorial, then turn right into Rosebarn Lane. Where its macadam surface narrows and turns left into a housing estate, take path TR29, a grassy lane, straight on to cross a stile, then follow a right-hand hedge straight on to the far end of the field. Here turn left for a few yards, then turn right over a stile and go straight across a field passing left of a telegraph pole to reach a hedge gap leading onto the towpath of the Aylesbury Arm of

the Grand Union Canal. Turn right onto this towpath and follow it for three-quarters of a mile, going under Dixon's Gap Bridge (if flooded, climbing the bank to a stiled road crossing) and passing four locks with a view of Marsworth Church ahead. At Marsworth the towpath (now MW16) goes under another bridge, passes a double lock and joins the main Grand Union Canal, then at Startop's End you finally climb a slope by the 'White Lion' to the B489 (Lower Icknield Way) where your starting point is a few yards to the right.

WALK 12:   Pitstone Hill

Length of Walk: (A) 7.4 miles / 11.9 Km
                     (B) 6.5 miles / 10.5 Km

Starting Point: Pitstone Hill car park.

Grid Ref: SP955149

Maps: OS Landranger Sheet 165
           OS Explorer Sheet 181 (or old Sheet 2)
           OS Pathfinder Sheet 1094 (SP81/91)
           Chiltern Society FP Map No. 19

How to get there / Parking: Pitstone Hill, 3 miles northeast
of Tring, may be reached from the western end of the town
by taking the B488 towards Dunstable for 3.7 miles. Just
after a narrow railway bridge with traffic lights, ignore a
right-hand turn for Tring Station and Aldbury, then at a
sharp left-hand bend, take a right turn also signposted to
Aldbury. After nearly half a mile, at the top of a rise and
opposite a footpath sign, turn right into an unmarked car
park.

Notes: Heavy nettle growth may be encountered in the
summer months particularly on paths IV1 and AB50.

Pitstone Hill, near the Buckinghamshire/Hertfordshire boundary,
rising to a height of 715 feet, marks the commencement of the
treeless downs of the northern end of the Chiltern Escarpment
which contrast with the wooded ridges further south. Since
the clearance of encroaching scrub by the Chiltern Society in
the late 1970s, regrowth has been controlled by the traditional
method of sheep-grazing. Just below the hill is the old village
of Pitstone, formerly known as Pightlesthorne, with its fine
thirteenth-century church. Beyond is the village of Pitstone
Green which grew considerably to house workers at the former
nearby cement works and is now joined to Ivinghoe with its
magnificent cruciform thirteenth-century church, fifteenth-
century inn, sixteenth-century town hall and other fine
buildings, while in the fields nearer to the hills stands a
restored postmill dating from 1627.

Both walks first take you along the ridge above these
villages, where superb views abound, with Walk A including
an additional loop to the summit of Ivinghoe Beacon, which

WALK 12

IVINGHOE

B 489

B 488

PITSTONE

Chalk Pit

Start   IV27
PT8

A/B

PT 12

PT 13

Ridgeway Path

Pitstone Hill

PT 13

AB 51

Aldbury Nowers

AB 46

AB 51   AB 50

N

0   1 mile

0   1 kilometre

A/B

Church Farm

Walk 9

Ivinghoe Beacon
IV 30
IV 26
IV 25

Gallows Hill

A   A

IV 2
IV 1
IV 27
A/B

Ridgeway

Steps Hill

Incombe Hole

Ward's Coombe

The Coombe

IV 1

Ward's Hurst Farm
IV 19

IV 13
Duncombe Terrace

Clipper Down

Beacon Road

Duncombe Farm
IV 13

BARLEY END   PT 11

AB 33

Stocks House

Little Stocks

Stocks Road

Bridgewater Monument

Walk 9
AB 32
AB 33

CP

'Greyhound'
AB 50

Aldbury Common

ALDBURY

'Valiant Trooper'

68

at 756 feet provides panoramic views in all directions. Both walks then lead you through woodland to cross a ridge and descend to the picturesque village of Aldbury in its sheltered valley, before returning via Aldbury Nowers and over the crest of Pitstone Hill to your starting point.

Starting from the vehicular entrance to the Pitstone Hill car park, cross the road and take the Ridgeway Path (PT8) through a kissing-gate opposite, following a grassy track (soon path IV27) straight on for a third of a mile to a gate and kissing-gate. Now take the grassy track straight on, soon skirting a deep, steep-sided coombe called Incombe Hole to your left and climbing steadily to reach a gate and stile near the top of Steps Hill. Do not cross the stile, but bear slightly left passing between the edge of the coombe and the fence to reach open downland. Here go straight on to a marker post at the edge of a belt of scrub, then follow the waymarked path through the scrub. On emerging onto open downland with superb views to your left, follow the right-hand fence straight on downhill to a kissing-gate. Now follow an obvious worn path over a rise and down again to a chalky track. Turn left onto this to reach a bend in Beacon Road, then step over a chain opposite.

Here **Walk B** turns right onto path IV1 following a grassy track towards a gate and kissing-gate. Now read the next paragraph. **Walk A** takes a chalky track (path IV2) straight on to cross a stile by a gate. Now bear half left along a grassy track across a field to the foot of a steep slope, then bear slightly left following a worn path steeply uphill to the crest of the ridge where wide views open out with Edlesborough with its prominent fourteenth-century church backed by Totternhoe Knolls ahead and the Dunstable Downs to your right. Here turn left onto path IV30 following the crest of the ridge uphill to a stile. Cross this, ignore a crossing path and go straight on uphill to the Beacon with its panoramic views. Now turn left onto path IV26 taking the left-hand of two worn paths downhill, soon joining path IV25. After a third of a mile you cross your outward route and follow a chalky path straight on to crossing path IV1. Turn left onto this, passing through a kissing-gate.

Here **Walks A and B** take path IV1 through the kissing-gate and follow a right-hand fence straight on to cross a stile by a gate, then continue to follow the right-hand fence to another stile. Now go straight on, passing right of a clump of hawthorn bushes, to reach a gate and kissing-gate into a wood called The Coombe. In the wood, follow a wide grassy track straight on for a quarter mile, then, at a fork, bear left, soon entering a cypress plantation. Go straight on through this plantation, then, having passed the corner of a left-hand field, keep left at a fork and follow a high wire-mesh fence straight on uphill. Where the high fence ends, ignore a rail-stile to your left and continue along the inside edge of the wood to its corner. Now cross a stile and follow a left-hand hedge straight on to a track junction by a gate at Ward's Hurst Farm. Here turn right onto path IV19, taking an obvious track straight on between farm buildings into a farmyard. Now bear left, then right onto a concrete farm road and follow this for a quarter mile to reach Beacon Road.

Turn right onto this road, then, after about 50 yards, turn left onto path IV13 into a wood called Duncombe Terrace. Just inside the wood, turn right onto a well-used path, then, after about 20 yards, fork left onto a branching path. At a T-junction by a twin-trunked tree, turn left onto a wider track and follow it downhill to reach a major crossing track. Here take an ill-defined path straight on downhill. In the bottom of the dip, ignore a crossing path and go straight on uphill to a stile into a field corner. Cross this and follow the outside edge of the wood straight on, disregarding a stile into it, then, by a corner of the wood, cross a stile and continue to follow its outside edge downhill with fine views towards Aldbury ahead. Where the edge of the wood begins to bear away to the right, leave it, bearing slightly left across the field and passing just left of an electricity and a telephone pole to reach the end of a road at Barley End by the gate to Duncombe Farm.

Cross this road and go through a gap by a stile opposite onto path PT11, bearing half left across a field to a concealed stile in the next hedge. Having crossed this, go straight across the next field towards a gate at the Hertfordshire boundary. Here ignore a crossing track and cross a stile beside the gate, then take path AB33 following a right-hand fence to cross a stile by a gate. Now follow a left-hand fence to a gate and stile, then take a drive straight on past a house to a road. Here go straight on over a stile and across a field to cross a stile under the tallest tree in the next hedge (where you join the reverse direction of Walk 9). Now turn right and follow the right-hand hedge to a corner of the field where you cross a stile and descend steps onto Stocks Road – BEWARE BLIND BEND – LISTEN FOR TRAFFIC! Turn left onto this road and follow it into the picturesque village of Aldbury.

On reaching the village centre, where the road forks, keep right (leaving Walk 9) passing the 'Greyhound', the village pond and seventeenth-century timbered manor house and the village green with its ancient wooden stocks which were in use till the 1830s. At a T-junction, turn right into Station Road leaving the green and passing the fourteenth-century church where the novelist, Mrs Humphry Ward, niece of Matthew Arnold and aunt of Aldous and Julian Huxley, who lived at Stocks House, was buried in 1920. Just past the church, turn right over a stile onto path AB50 and go straight across a field to a gate and stile. Cross the stile, then bear slightly left to a kissing-gate by the corner of a modern barn at Church Farm. Now follow a path between the barn and a hedge then cross two stiles and go straight on along a fenced path to a kissing-gate into a fenced bridleway. Cross the bridleway and a stile opposite, then take a gravel path straight on across a golf course to a wooden signpost. Here keep straight on along a grassy path, climbing gently to reach a gap in bushes ahead. Now follow a right-hand hedge uphill to reach the corner of a wood. Here cross a stile and a fenced permissive bridleway, then go through a kissing-gate into the wood and follow an obvious winding path until you reach a sunken way (path AB46). Turn left onto this and after about 40 yards, turn right onto path AB51 (the Ridgeway Path). Now follow its obvious waymarked course for two-thirds of a mile through a mixture of woodland and scrubland on Aldbury Nowers with fine views to your left across the Tring Gap in places, until a kissing gate at the county boundary leads you out onto the open downland of Pitstone Hill. Here take path PT13, continuing to follow an ancient earthwork which you have been following for some distance, to the top of Pitstone Hill. Near the corner of a fence, leave the earthwork and follow the fence straight on along the ridge for over half a mile, ignoring the stile of a crossing path and later joining path PT12, to reach a stile into the end of the car park.

WALK 13: Aldbury Common

Length of Walk: 7.1 miles / 11.4 Km

Starting Point: Bridgewater Monument turning off B4506 at Aldbury Common.

Grid Ref: SP979128

Maps: OS Landranger Sheets 165 & 166
OS Explorer Sheet 181
OS Pathfinder Sheets 1094 (SP81/91)
(or old Explorer Sheet 2) & 1095 (TL01/11)
Chiltern Society FP Map No. 19

How to get there / Parking: The starting point, 3 miles north of Berkhamsted, may be reached from the town by taking the A4251 to Northchurch, then turning right onto the B4506 and following it for 2.7 miles. About two-thirds of a mile past the Aldbury turn, turn left onto the macadam road to the Bridgewater Monument and park as soon as possible.

Notes: Heavy nettle growth may be encountered in summer particularly on parts of bridleway LG10 and path LG12.

Aldbury Common is one of a belt of several mostly wooded commons extending from the outskirts of Berkhamsted to Aldbury village and across the Bucks boundary to the Chiltern escarpment. When the Ashridge Estate was sold in 1929, a large area of these commons was acquired by the National Trust which has done much to facilitate public access. Ashridge House, which can be seen at the eastern end of Prince's Riding (where the car park is located), was commissioned by the third Duke of Bridgewater before his death in 1803 to replace a mediaeval house which had formerly been a monastery. Designed in the neo-Gothic style by James Wyatt and his nephew, Sir Jeffry Wyatville, the house was completed in about 1820. At the other end of the Riding, which forms part of the landscaping carried out by Capability Brown and amended by Repton, is the Bridgewater Monument erected in 1832 in memory of the third Duke of Bridgewater who is noted as 'the Father of the English canal system'.

The walk first explores parts of the wooded Aldbury and Berkhamsted Commons before crossing Golden Valley to the

south-eastern end of Little Gaddesden. From here it takes you
across a small valley to Hudnall Common, another National
Trust property, then downhill to the Beds boundary in the
Gade valley, before returning via the north-western end of
Little Gaddesden and Ashridge Golf Course to your starting
point.

Starting from the entrance to the road to the Bridgewater Monument,
take the B4506 southwards for a few yards, then turn right onto
bridleway AB21, a grassy path into the woods. Follow it straight on
for a third of a mile, ignoring four crossing paths. On reaching path
AB12, a wide waymarked crossing track, turn left onto it. At a five-
way track junction go straight on, at one point passing a field to your
left. Just before a left-hand pond, turn left onto a crossing track
(bridleway AB14) briefly joining the Chiltern Way. After about 100
yards at a fork, leaving the Chiltern Way again, take the waymarked
right-hand lesser alternative (path AB15) and follow it straight on,
passing left of some large beech trees, to reach the B4506.

Cross this road and turn right onto its walkable verge to reach a
road junction. Here turn left onto bridleway NC33, a rough track into
a large clearing. Go straight on along the right-hand edge of the
clearing. At its far side take a grassy path straight on through the
trees. Ignore a branching path to the right and on reaching a wide
crossing track, turn left onto it. After a few yards at a crossways turn
right onto a wide grassy track (still NC33) and follow it straight on for
a third of a mile. Just past Little Coldharbour Farm, join a stony track
and follow it straight on to a track junction by Coldharbour Farm.
Here bear slightly right, crossing a track leading to the farm and
taking a rough bridle track straight on into the woods. At a three-way
fork at the bottom of a slope, take the middle option (bridleway NC48)
bearing half left and follow this track out to the edge of a field. Here
bear half left again and follow the outside edge of the woods for nearly
half a mile to a corner of the field then go straight on through
woodland to reach the Ashridge road.

Cross this road and take path LG7, a macadam drive opposite.
Follow this uphill, ignoring a right-hand fork, until you reach a house
called Rodinghead. Here leave the drive and take a fenced track
straight on between fields to cross a stile by a gate. Now go straight on
downhill across a large field heading for and passing through a clump
of trees. Here keep straight on downhill into Golden Valley passing
through a bridlegate at one point and heading for a tall beech tree at
the edge of Cromer Wood left of a fenced pumping station compound.
Go straight on into the wood, climbing the steep slope diagonally until
you reach an old iron gatepost at the corner of a wall. Now take a

sunken path uphill beside the wall through laurel bushes to reach Nettleden Road at Little Gaddesden.

Cross this road and turn right onto its pavement. Just past Shepherd's Cottage, turn left through white gates onto bridleway LG10 into Home Farm. By the farmhouse gates bear slightly left off the concrete drive into a narrow bridleway leading between a fence and a wall to a bridlegate. Now turn right then immediately left round the end of a stable block, then go straight on through the left-hand of two gates leaving the farm and taking a fenced track downhill. In the valley bottom do not go through the gate ahead, but turn left and follow the fenced bridleway to the corner of the right-hand field. Here turn right and climb a hill to enter a copse at the edge of Hudnall Common.

Just inside the copse, ignore two lesser branching paths to the left and follow the bridleway straight on through the copse and some scrub to reach a road. Now take bridleway LG10 straight on across open common, with views across the Gade valley towards Studham ahead, heading for single oak then continuing straight on to reach a well worn track into scrubland. Take this track straight on downhill through the scrub ignoring two crossing paths. After a quarter mile, at a fork bear left to join Hudnall Lane near the Bedfordshire boundary.

Cross this road and take chalky path LG15 opposite, turning left alongside the road and gradually bearing away from it through scrubland. At a fork keep left, soon emerging onto open common. Bear half right across the common to the far right-hand corner, then take a waymarked path straight on through a narrow strip of woodland to an access road to houses along the edge of the common. Bear slightly right onto this road (path LG14) and at a right-hand bend by the entrance to Meadow Farm, fork left onto a path signposted to Little Gaddesden. Take this path straight on between hedges to a kissing-gate into a field, then follow the right-hand hedge straight on to cross a stile (where you meet the route of Walk 17 and join the Chiltern Way). Here take path LG12 bearing half left across a large field, passing right of an oak tree to reach a stile about 80 yards right of the far corner. Now go straight on to cross a stile just right of the corner of the next field, then continue straight on to cross a stile onto Church Road, which leads to Little Gaddesden's fifteenth-century church (described in Walk 17). Bear slightly left across this road and another stile, then bear half left across a paddock, passing the rear corner of a garden to reach a kissing-gate near the far corner of the paddock. Go through this and follow a narrow fenced path round the backs of gardens then diagonally across a field to a kissing-gate in front of a red-roofed house at Little Gaddesden.

Go through this and turn right onto a road then immediately left onto path LG5 through the 'Bridgewater Arms' car park to a stile in

its rear fence. Now follow a fenced path downhill to a macadam access road. Cross this and bear slightly left into a hedged path, soon crossing a further drive and continuing straight on until you enter a wood. Here go straight on uphill, soon crossing a golf tee and a track, then keep straight on through woodland and between garden fences to reach a macadam drive. Turn left onto this, then at a T-junction turn right, then immediately left onto a macadam drive (still LG5). Go straight on past a bungalow called Pitstone Copse, then at the far end of its garden leave the drive and keep straight on, following the edge of a left-hand copse across the golf course, then continuing straight on between the clubhouse and several greens to a worn track leading into woodland ahead. On reaching a track junction by Old Park Lodge, bear slightly left passing left of the house. By the far end of its garden, leaving the Chiltern Way, bear half right onto path LG6 leaving the track and crossing the golf course diagonally, passing right of a green and aiming for a single birch tree at the edge of the fairway. Pass right of this tree then go straight on through a belt of trees to reach Prince's Riding, which gives you a brief glimpse to your left of Ashridge House. Cross this ride and take a woodland path straight on, passing through a clearing near a building and soon emerging onto a macadam drive. Turn right onto this and follow it to a gateway by Thunderdell Lodge onto the B4506. Cross this and turn right onto a rough path along its verge back to your starting point.

Length of Walk: (A)   8.8 miles / 14.2 Km
                         (B)   6.2 miles / 10.0 Km
                         (C)   5.0 miles / 8.0 Km

Starting Point: (A/B) Unmarked car park in Dodds Lane,
                         Piccott's End.
                         (C)   Corner Farm road junction,
                         Gaddesden Row.

Grid Ref;   (A/B) TL052095
                         (C)   TL066117

Maps: OS Landranger Sheet 166
            OS Explorer Sheet 182
            OS Pathfinder Sheets 1095 (TL01/11) (all)
            & 1119 (TL00/10) (A/B only)
            Chiltern Society FP Map No. 20 (all Walk B / part of
            Walks A/C only)

How to get there / Parking: **(A/B)** Piccott's End, on
the northern edge of Hemel Hempstead, may be reached
from the town centre by taking the A4146 towards
Leighton Buzzard to a roundabout at its junction with
the A4147. Here turn right onto the A4147, then at
the next roundabout turn left into Piccott's End. Go
straight on through the village for half a mile. Where
the right-hand houses end, turn right into Dodds Lane
and follow it for some 300 yards, then turn left through
a hedge gap into a small unmarked car park.
(C) Corner Farm, Gaddesden Row, 3 miles north of
Hemel Hempstead, may be reached from the town by
taking the A4146 towards Leighton Buzzard to the
'Red Lion' at Water End. Here turn right onto the road
signposted to Flamstead and Markyate and follow it for
1.8 miles to a T-junction at Gaddesden Row. Now turn
right and follow the road for 0.8 miles to a road junction
by Corner Farm, where you can park on the wide grass
verges.

Notes: Heavy nettle growth may be encountered in places in
summer on all three walks, while bridleway GG42 on Walks
A & C may be very muddy in places even in dry weather.

0 _____ 1mile

0 _____ 1kilometre

Piccott's End, on the River Gade, only a mile north of the centre of Hemel Hempstead, is still an attractive village in a relatively unspoilt setting despite the fact that the town's rapidly expanding housing estates have covered the tops of the hills on either side of the valley. In 1953 mediaeval wall-paintings were discovered in a fifteenth-century cottage in the village called Hall House, which also has a priest hide and a mediaeval well.

All three alternative walks pass close to Gaddesden Place on the slopes of the Gade valley above Water End. This house was originally built for the Halsey family in 1768–1773 by James Wyatt, who later designed Ashridge, but had to be largely rebuilt after a disastrous fire in 1905. In addition, Walks A and C explore the peaceful plateau to the east of the Gade valley, while Walks A and B cross and recross the scenic Gade valley visiting the picturesque hamlet of Water End and exploring the hills to the west

Walks A and B start from the unmarked car park in Dodds Lane, Piccott's End, and take path GG55 leading out of the car park up a rough hedged lane, the right-hand hedge of which soon peters out. Where the track turns right across the field, continue along it to the corner of a hedge. Now go through a hedge gap and follow a winding right-hand hedge straight on uphill to cross a stile with views behind of Hemel Hempstead and the Gade valley. Here follow the right-hand hedge straight on, then, where it turns right, go straight on across the field to a stile by a tree in front of the farmhouse at Wood Farm. Do **not** cross this stile, but turn left onto path GG56 crossing the field to an oak tree. Here go straight on, joining the edge of Varney's Wood and following it, at one point turning left, to double-gates and a stile at a corner of the wood. Cross this stile and continue along the edge of the wood. Where this turns right, follow a field boundary straight on to reach crossing bridleway GG39 by the end of a belt of trees. For **Walk A** now omit the next paragraph.

Walk B turns left here onto bridleway GG39 and follows its winding course downhill beside a left-hand hedge for a quarter mile to the bottom corner of the field. Now turn right through a hedge gap onto path GG38 and follow a right-hand hedge uphill, eventually with a young plantation to your left. Just before reaching a mature copse ahead, turn left and follow the edge of the copse through the plantation to a hedge gap where there is a fine view behind you towards Hemel Hempstead. Go through this gap and take a grassy track uphill to some garages. Here turn left onto a stony track which leads you to a road at Briden's Camp. Turn right onto this winding road and follow it for a third of a mile, passing the 'Crown & Sceptre' and rounding first a sharp left-hand, then a sharp right-hand bend. Some 130 yards beyond the right-hand bend, turn left onto path GG22, the concrete road towards Home Farm. Where its concrete ends, turn left over a stile by double-gates onto path GG21 rejoining **Walk A**. Now omit the next four paragraphs.

Walk A turns right onto bridleway GG39, joining **Walk C**, then **Walks A and C** follow the outside edge of the tree-belt. At the far end of the tree-belt, continue through a hedge gap and follow a left-hand hedge straight on through three fields for nearly a mile with views of the modern outskirts of Hemel Hempstead to your right. Near the far end of the third field, descend into a sunken gully to join Cupid Green Lane at a sharp bend. Now follow this narrow road straight on downhill and up again for a quarter mile to reach the Corner Farm road junction at Gaddesden Row.

At the Corner Farm road junction **(the start of Walk C), Walks A and C** take the Redbourn road straight on. After about 330 yards, opposite double-gates, turn left onto fenced bridleway GG42, then turn immediately left over a stile onto fenced path GG42a. Follow this path beside the bridleway, turning right then left. On reaching another stile, cross it, the bridleway and a further stile opposite. Now continue between fences, turning left by a house and passing a paddock to reach a stile back onto bridleway GG42 at the edge of a wood. Take the bridleway straight on to the far side of the wood, then by a metal gate to your right, take a green lane straight on (joining the reverse direction of Walk 15), soon passing Long Wood and a field to your left and entering Round Spring Wood. Take the bridleway through the wood soon transferring through a gap in the right-hand hedge to the other side of the hedge and continuing between it and a fence to Upper Wood Farm.

Here (leaving Walk 15 again) turn left onto a farm road (path GG30) and follow it for a third of a mile to the Gaddesden Row road near the 'Old Chequers'. Turn right onto this road, then at a junction, turn left onto the Water End and Hemel Hempstead road and follow it for a third of a mile. Just past the bottom of a dip, turn right through a hedge gap onto path GG32 following a right-hand hedge to the far side of the field. Here go straight on into the middle of a crossing avenue of lime trees, then turn left onto path GG34, a grassy track along the avenue. Where the track bears left and leaves the avenue, follow it, immediately forking right onto path GG33 along the outside edge of the avenue, then the edge of London Wood. On reaching the gravel road to Home Farm (path GG22), turn left onto it. Just before it becomes concreted, **Walk A** turns right over a stile by double-gates onto path GG21, then omit the next paragraph.

Walk C takes path GG22 straight on along the concrete road, then turns right onto a public road and follows it for a third of a mile. Having passed the 'Crown and Sceptre', at a sharp right-hand bend, turn left onto path GG38, a stony track beside some farm cottages with a fine view down the Gade valley to Hemel Hempstead. On reaching some garages, turn right onto a grassy track and follow it past a copse to a hedge gap. Go through this gap, then turn left and follow the edge of the copse downhill through a young plantation to reach a hedge in a dip. Here turn right and follow the near side of the hedge downhill to a hedge gap in the bottom corner of the field. Go through this gap, then turn left onto well-worn bridleway GG39 and follow its winding course uphill for a quarter mile to rejoin **Walk A** by a belt of trees. Now go back four paragraphs.

Walks A and B now take path GG21 bearing slightly right across parkland with a view to your right of Home Farm, a good example of a technologically advanced Victorian farm, to cross a stile just right of some large oaks where the imposing façade of Gaddesden Place comes into view ahead. Now bear slightly right across a parkland field, heading for an oak tree flanking the right-hand edge of a wide gap in the trees right of Gaddesden Place. Here, joining the Chiltern Way, go through gates and bear half left, soon with fine views of Great Gaddesden and the Gade valley and of Gaddesden Place behind you, passing just right of a cattle trough and left of a large hollybush then between a conifer and an oak to a stile. Now cross the corner of another field to a further stile with a fine view of Water End with its picturesque seventeenth-century brick and timber cottages ahead. Here bear slightly left, aiming for an ash tree just left of a white cottage to reach the corner of a garden fence. Follow the fence straight on past the cottage towards the road to a stile onto the garden path and a handgate leading onto the A4146 at Water End.

Cross this road and turn right, then turn immediately left onto path GG66 leading between garden walls to two stiles. Having crossed these, bear half right, following a fence at first to reach a footbridge over the River Gade. At the far end of this bridge, turn left (still on GG66) and follow the river to a footbridge over a small watercourse, then go straight on, gradually deviating from the river to reach a stile. Cross this and bear slightly right to join a right-hand fence then follow it, ignoring a stile in it, to reach two gates and stiles leading to Nettleden Road. Turn right onto this road, then after about 60 yards, turn left through a kissing-gate onto path GG63. Now go straight on uphill, passing left of a dead beech tree, to reach a track into Heizdin's Wood. Before entering the wood, turn round for a fine view across the valley then follow the track uphill through the wood ignoring a crossing path. On leaving the wood, bear half right across a field to the left-hand of two small oak trees, then bear slightly left to reach the end of a hedge. Here bear half left onto path GG62 along the near side of the hedge to a kissing-gate. Go through this, then bear slightly right into a fenced lane leading to Water End Road on the edge of Potten End.

Turn right onto this road and at a right-hand bend, turn left through a small gate onto fenced path GG59. On crossing a stile, follow the sporadic right-hand hedge straight on, then after about 50 yards, by an oak tree, go through a gap in the hedge and walk downhill between it and a wire fence to a stile at the bottom. Cross this and turn left (now on path HH17), then turn right over a stile by a gate onto a fenced farm track uphill to Boxted Farm. Where the track ends, go straight on through a fence gap by gates and continue ahead until you reach a wooden fence. Now turn right and follow this fence, turning right and later left through a hedge gap to a kissing-gate onto the farm drive. Leaving the Chiltern Way, turn right onto this, then immediately left through a kissing-gate onto path HH18 and bear half left, following a left-hand fence to cross a stile. Now follow a right-hand fence straight on to a stile at the far end of the field. Turn right over this and follow the left-hand hedge through two fields to a road on the edge of Hemel Hempstead.

Turn left onto this road, then by an anti-vehicle barrier, fork left, soon crossing a stile by a gate onto path HH13. Now follow the edge of a field straight on beside gardens. At its far end, cross a stile and continue between a hedge and a fence. Where the fence ends, follow the outside edge of Warnersend Wood, then a right-hand hedge straight on. At the far end of the field, bear slightly right to pass through a squeeze-stile, then continue along a fenced path. On reaching a bend in a track, join it and follow it straight on past a wood and farm buildings to reach a macadam drive, then continue along this soon reaching the A4146. Cross this road and go straight on across a bridge over the Gade to reach the village street in Piccott's End. Turn left onto this and after some 130 yards, turn right into Dodds Lane. About 30 yards up the lane, where a left-hand hedge begins, leave the road and take path HH10 following the back of the roadside hedge to a hedge gap into the car park.

WALK 15: Redbourn

Length of Walk: 9.1 miles / 14.6 Km

Starting Point: Car park near cricket pitch on Redbourn Common.

Grid Ref: TL103119

Maps: OS Landranger Sheet 166
OS Explorer Sheet 182
OS Pathfinder Sheet 1095 (TL01/11)

How to get there / Parking: Redbourn, 4 miles northeast of Hemel Hempstead, may be reached from the town by taking the B487. After passing under the M1, turn left onto a road signposted to Church End and follow it straight on for half a mile to a car park to your left on Redbourn Common.

Notes: Heavy nettle growth may be encountered in the summer months, particularly on path FS45, while bridleway GG42 may be very muddy in places even in dry weather.

Redbourn in the Ver valley, the name of which means 'reedy stream' suggesting that the area was once marshy, is set around an extensive and very attractive common where cricket has been played since 1666. At the southwestern end of the common is the original village known as Church End where a street of picturesque cottages leads to the twelfth-century church, noted for its carved oak rood screen dating from 1478. East of the common is the village High Street on the line of a Roman road called Watling Street. This road, which has now been bypassed by the A5183 (formerly A5), was particularly busy in the eighteenth and early nineteenth centuries when it formed the main stagecoach road from London to Birmingham, Liverpool and Holyhead and thus inns and other buildings sprang up here during this period to service the coaches. Before the construction of the M1, the age of the motor-car brought another flood of heavy traffic to the High Street, but with the bypass it is now relatively peaceful again. Finally, north of the common is an area of modern housing estates which have swelled the population to 6,000, but nevertheless this is only a small development in comparison with what

83

WALK 15

84

would have occurred if the one-time plan to make Redbourn the site of a new town had been implemented.

The walk takes you out of Redbourn over the hills to the west of the Ver valley to the hilltop village of Flamstead. From here, it leads you southwestwards through remote hill country to near the scattered community of Gaddesden Row before returning through equally remote hill country to Redbourn.

Starting from the back of the car park on Redbourn Common, turn right onto macadam path RB17 within a fine avenue of lime trees (briefly interrupted on one side by the cricket pitch) and follow it to Lybury Lane. Turn left onto this road and follow it straight on for over a third of a mile, crossing the common and passing through a housing estate. On reaching an open green in the middle of the estate, turn right onto a road round the edge of the green, then take the first road leaving the green to reach a T-junction. Here turn left into Snatchup, then at a second T-junction, cross a road called Long Cutt and take hedged path RB51 straight on to a gate into a recreation ground. Enter the recreation ground, then take a macadam path straight on across it, then between houses to reach the end of a residential road. Take this road straight on, then turn right into the first right-hand cul-de-sac. At its far end turn left onto a macadam path, then immediately right onto crossing macadam path RB52. At a further T-junction of paths turn left onto enclosed path RB3 and follow it straight on for 150 yards, ignoring a branching path to your left until a fence forces you to turn left into a field. Now follow a right-hand hedge, almost immediately turning right. Where the hedge ends, ignore a branching path to your right and bear slightly left, following a right-hand fence. Where the fence turns right, go straight on along a grassy path, later passing through a gap in the vestiges of a hedge and following the right-hand side of a line of trees. On reaching a more solid hedge, keep left of this and follow it straight on to the boundary fence of the M1. Here bear half right, following the M1 fence through a wood and a field to a gate and stile onto Redding Lane, where you obtain a fine view of the Ver valley.

Turn left onto this road, crossing a bridge over the M1, then just before reaching Norrington End Farm, turn left over a stile by a gate onto path RB5 and go straight across a field to the corner of a hedge. Here take path RB3a turning right through a hedge gap and following a sporadic right-hand hedge past the farm with a fine view of the Ver valley ahead. Where the hedge swings right, bear half left across the field to concealed stiles in the left-hand hedge. Cross these and turn right onto path FS23, following the right-hand hedge downhill. Where this hedge turns right, go straight on downhill across two fields to a stile at the far side of the second field. Now bear slightly left uphill to a stile under a crab-tree to the right of the top left-hand corner of the field. Do **not** cross this stile, but instead turn left onto path FS24 and follow the right-hand hedge to the corner of the field. Here enter a hedged lane and follow it straight on to Delmerend Lane. Turn right onto this road, then, after about 100 yards, turn left onto path FS25, another hedged lane. On emerging in a field, follow the right-hand hedge straight on to a kissing-gate into a fenced alleyway leading to a residential road in Flamstead.

Flamstead, a corruption of 'Verlamstead', is an attractive village set on a hilltop above the Ver valley. The village, when seen from afar, is dominated by its magnificent twelfth-century church with its massive tower containing Roman bricks and its interior boasting some fine mediaeval murals and later marble monuments.

Turn right onto this road and follow it round left- and right-hand bends, then turn left through a kissing-gate into the churchyard. Here, if wishing to visit one of the village pubs or look at the attractive village centre, take the right-hand path (FS29) passing right of the church. Otherwise, take path FS30, the left-hand of the three paths through the churchyard, to a gate and gap leading to Trowley Hill Road. Turn left onto this road, then immediately right onto path FS32, a fenced alleyway leading you out past a housing estate into a field. Now go straight on across the field, passing a telegraph pole and then heading for a hedge gap left of an ash tree in tall bushes ahead. Go through this gap and turn left onto a narrow road called Pietley Hill. At a left-hand bend, turn right over a stile onto path FS37, bearing slightly right downhill to cross a stile at the bottom, then continue uphill to reach the top hedge, where you turn right and follow the near side of the hedge to a gap in a field corner leading into Wood End Lane where there is a fine view behind you across the valley to Flamstead.

Turn right onto this road then just after Scratch Wood begins to your left, turn right over a stile by a gate and take path FS45 bearing slightly left across a field to the near corner of a wood called Yewtree Spring. Here keep right of the wood and follow its outside edge to a stile into it. Turn left over this and follow the waymarked path through this wood, carpeted in bluebells in April and May, to reach a stile at the far corner into a field. Here bear slightly right across the field, with views ahead across these remote hills towards the distant Bedfordshire village of Studham, to a stile in a hedge just right of a corner of the field. Cross this and turn left, following a left-hand hedge and fence. On nearing Little Woodend Cottages, where the left-hand fence diverges from the hedge, cross a stile in the fence and keep left of a shed to join a drive by the cottages. Take this drive straight on to reach a road then turn left onto it and follow it through Newlands Wood. Just after a slight left-hand bend turn right over a stile onto path FS46 and bear slightly left across a field passing the corner of a copse called Abel's Grove to reach a hedge gap in the far corner of the field. Here turn left into a green lane and follow it to a right-hand bend, then turn left through a hedge gap onto path GG28 following a grassy track beside a right-hand hedge for over a quarter mile to a road. Turn right onto this road then after about 80 yards turn left through a hedge gap onto bridleway GG29 following a fenced track beside a right-hand hedge to Upper Wood Farm.

Here, on reaching a farm road (path GG30), if wanting refreshments, turn right onto it to reach the 'Old Chequers', Gaddesden Row, in just over a third of a mile. Otherwise, join the reverse direction of Walk 14, crossing the farm road and taking bridleway GG42, a fenced track right of a metal gate, straight on beside a right-hand hedge. On reaching the corner of Round Spring Wood, follow the track into and through the wood to reach a field. Here follow the fenced bridleway straight on beside a left-hand hedge to enter Long Wood, then continue through it and along a hedged lane until you reach the beginning of a third wood, left of the lane. Leaving Walk 14, turn left here over a stile by an iron gate onto path GG41, following the outside edge of the wood straight on. Where the edge of the wood turns right, go straight on downhill to reach the edge of Greenlane Wood, then turn right onto path GG41a following it. At the far end of the wood, turn left through a hedge gap onto path FS41 following the outside edge of the wood, then a left-hand hedge uphill. Where the hedge turns left, bear slightly right across the field, heading for an ash tree in the hedge ahead, to reach a hedge gap into Green Lane. Bear slightly right into this appropriately-named lane and follow it passing a cottage to reach a T-junction with a macadam road.

Here turn right and follow the road for some 60 yards. Just past a telegraph pole turn left onto path FS40 following a crop-break, later a hedge, for some 700 yards to reach New Wood. Now join a track and follow it straight on for over half a mile, ignoring all branching tracks and eventually reaching a macadam farm road near Flamsteadbury Farm. Turn right onto this road (bridleway FS39, later RB23) and follow it past the farm and over the M1 into Redbourn. On reaching the village, take this road called Flamsteadbury Lane straight on to Redbourn Common. Here take West Common straight on then just before Church End to your right, turn left onto macadam path RB17 within the avenue of lime trees and follow it back to your starting point.

WALK 16:   Markyate

Length of Walk: 4.9 miles / 7.9 Km
Starting Point: 'Sun Inn', Markyate.
Grid Ref: TL062164
Maps: OS Landranger Sheet 166
            OS Explorer Sheet 182
            OS Pathfinder Sheet 1095 (TL01/11)
            Chiltern Society FP Map No. 21

How to get there / Parking: Markyate, 3.5 miles southwest
of Luton, may be reached by leaving the M1 at Junction 9
(Flamstead). Now take the A5 towards Dunstable and fork
left onto the road into the village. On reaching the village
centre, find a suitable on-street parking place in one of the
side-streets.

Markyate, formerly known variously as Markyate Street or
even Market Street, grew up as a long straggle of mainly
eighteenth-century buildings along Watling Street, the Roman
road from Dover via London, Verulamium (St. Albans) and
Durocobrivae (Dunstable) to the West Midlands, and has only
in recent years spread out substantially from this road.
Although the village was bypassed by the modern A5 in 1957, a
number of old coaching inns still bear witness to the fact that
the main road used to run through the village. To the north of
Markyate is its Georgian parish church built in 1724 in a park
known as Markyate Cell because it was in mediaeval times the
site of a nunnery. The present house with this name, built in
1825, replaced an earlier one which, in the seventeenth
century, had been the home of a widow named Lady Katherine
Ferrers. Legend has it that she became a highwayman and
later haunted both the old house and the A5. Earlier in the
same century, the village also featured in national events
when the servant of Ambrose Rookwood, one of the
conspirators in the Gunpowder Plot, was arrested at the 'Sun
Inn' in 1605. Some 130 years later, Markyate was also the
location of a boarding school attended by the young William
Cowper of Berkhamsted who was later to achieve fame as a
poet.

The walk, which includes some fine views, first takes you out of Markyate and the Ver valley and explores the hill country on the Bedfordshire boundary to the north of the village before recrossing the Ver valley near Kensworth Lynch and following the top of its southern slope to Markyate.

Starting from the 'Sun Inn' in Markyate High Street, follow the High Street southeastwards for about 60 yards, then turn left into Hicks Road and follow it out to the A5. Cross the main road by way of a footbridge and at the far end of it, turn left down a flight of steps and cross the extension of Hicks Road. Now take a macadam road opposite, called The Ridings, straight on to a gate and stile at the end of the road. Cross the stile and take path MY7, bearing slightly right across a field to cross a stile at the left-hand end of a hedge. Now bear half left across the next field to the near corner of a garden hedge. Keep left of this hedge and follow it straight on, then, where the hedge turns right, continue straight on to join a drive which leads you out to the B4540.

Cross this road, turn right onto its pavement and follow it for a third of a mile, ignoring a side-turning and passing a row of bungalows. Opposite a water-tower in the trees to your right, turn left over a stile onto path MY8 and bear half right across a field, heading between two electricity poles ahead to reach a stile. Cross this and bear half right heading for the distant Caddington Church to cross a stile at the county boundary at the far side of the field. Here turn left onto an unnumbered path crossing another stile and following a left-hand fence to a stile at the far side of the field. Cross this and follow a fenced path, ignoring a gap in the left-hand fence and entering a right-hand field. Now take path CA22 following the left-hand hedge straight on to a gate and rails, through which you climb to reach Pipers Lane on the edge of the Bedfordshire village of Aley Green.

Turn right onto this road and follow it through Aley Green to a T-junction by Piper's Farm. Here turn left and after some 130 yards, turn left again over a footbridge and through a hedge gap onto path CA19, following a right-hand hedge uphill at first then on the level. On reaching a corner of the field, turn right onto path CA18, keeping left of a sporadic hedge and following it through two fields with views of Caddington to your right ahead. At the far end of the second field, do **not** go through the hedge gap, but instead turn left onto path CA17 and follow a right-hand hedge for a third of a mile to a gap by gates into Millfield Lane. Turn right onto this road, then just past a white house, turn left through a gap by a gate onto path CA17/MY10, following a left-hand hedge to reach a copse. Go straight on through the copse, then continue across a field past an oak tree to a gap in the next hedge. Drop down though this gap and go straight on downhill with views across both spurs of the Ver valley ahead to cross a stile just left of an ash tree. Now continue straight on downhill to a gate and stile in the bottom left-hand corner of the field leading to the A5.

Here cross the A5 bearing slightly left to a hedge gap opposite the entrance to a nursery, then take signposted path KN12 over some low rails and straight on uphill across a field to reach a marker post at the hilltop. Now turn left and head slightly left of a single electricity pole on the skyline to cross a footbridge under a chestnut tree over a ditch, which is all there is of the River Ver near its source at Kensworth Lynch.

Cross this bridge and turn right onto the B4540. After a few yards turn left through a concealed swing-gate left of double gates onto path KN13, a farm track which climbs steadily. Where the track turns right and there are fine views of the Ver valley to your left, follow a left-hand line of trees, then a hedge straight on. About 100 yards short of the far end of the field, turn left through a hedge gap onto path KN2 and bear half right across the corner of a field to reach another hedge gap. Go through this gap and take path MY13 following a grassy track straight on beside a left-hand hedge, with views ahead of Flamstead on a distant hilltop and through gaps in the hedge of the Ver valley including Markyate Cell in its wooded park. At the far end of the field, go through a hedge gap and follow a left-hand fence straight on beneath a power line past Manor Farm to a kissing-gate at the far end of the field. Go through this gate and follow the left-hand hedge past a playing field, the village hall and a children's playground into an alleyway leading to Cavendish Road in Markyate. Turn left onto this road, following it downhill to the High Street, then turn right to reach your starting point.

WALK 16

CADDINGTON

Length of Walk: 6.5 miles / 10.4 Km
Starting Point: Crossroads by 'Red Lion', Studham.
Grid Ref: TL023158
Maps: OS Landranger Sheets 165 & 166
           OS Explorer Sheets 181 (or old Sheet 2) & 182
           OS Pathfinder Sheets 1094 (SP81/91) & 1095 (TL01/11)
           Chiltern Society FP Maps Nos. 19 & 20
How to get there / Parking: Studham, 4 miles south of
   Dunstable, may be reached from the town by taking the
   B489 towards Aston Clinton, then forking left onto the
   B4541 towards Whipsnade and the Downs and following
   it for 2.2 miles. At its junction with the B4540, take the
   Studham and Hemel Hempstead road straight on for 1.6
   miles, then, at a crossroads in the village by the village
   hall, 'Red Lion' and war memorial clocktower, there is a
   small car park on the left. If full, turn right into Church
   Road and find a suitable on-street parking place.
Notes: Heavy nettle growth may be encountered in places in
   the summer months.

Studham, the southernmost village in Bedfordshire, nestles in
a hollow in the backland of the Dunstable Downs, surrounded
by an extensive upland plateau. Until 1897, the village, which
was once a centre of the straw-plait industry and was one of
the early strongholds of Nonconformity, in fact, straddled the
Hertfordshire boundary and it was only then that the southern
half of its extensive common and many of its scattered farms
and cottages were transferred to the same county as the
church and village centre. The cement-rendered thirteenth-
century church, which is somewhat isolated and hidden at the
end of its cul-de-sac lane, has a surprisingly beautiful interior
with fine carved stone capitals and an unusual carved Norman
font pre-dating the present building.
   The walk, which traverses three counties, leads you first
westwards across the plateau past the church to descend the
escarpment to the Buckinghamshire village of Dagnall, before
turning south and climbing through quiet woodland to the
hilltop Hertfordshire village of Little Gaddesden. You then

return northeastwards to Studham, on the way skirting Hudnall and crossing the upper reaches of the Gade Valley. Although basically an open walk with fine viewpoints, some pleasant woodland provides variety.

Starting from the crossroads by the 'Red Lion' at Studham, take Church Road, then turn right onto path ST18 striking off between Studham Methodist Church and a road called Swannell's Wood. Now go through a gap by a gate and follow a left-hand hedge through two fields, joining Walk 18 in the second field. At the far end of this field, take path ST19 following a grassy track which bears half right to the corner of a hedge and tree belt concealing Studham churchyard then bears half left and follows the churchyard hedge to a crossing track. Here take path ST21 straight on over a stile, following a right-hand fence past two large trees, then bear slightly left diverging gradually from the fence to reach a stile and footbridge into a wood called Church Grove.

Inside the wood, disregard a crossing bridleway (the Chiltern Way, onto which Walk 18 turns right) and follow a well-defined track straight on until you reach a waymarked T-junction. Here turn right onto path ST23 and follow this track to a crossing track at the edge of the wood. Now go straight on, leaving the wood by a gap to the right of the horse-jump ahead. Follow the edge of the wood, later a left-hand hedge, straight on to a hedge gap at the far end of the field. Go through this and bear slightly right across the next field to a concealed hedge gap just beyond a slight kink in the right-hand hedge. Go through this gap onto Buckinghamshire path ED15, then bear slightly right across a golf course, keeping right of a green and fairway ahead to reach a marker post in the trees ahead. Here ignore a branching path to your right and bear slightly left following the left-hand edge of a tree belt. At the far end of this tree belt, bear slightly left passing left of a tee to reach the right-hand end of a short section of hedge, then go straight on, passing just left of a cherry tree and crossing a tee to a stile into woodland. Here follow a fenced path straight on downhill, ignoring a crossing drive and continuing for some 350 yards to a stile. Cross this and follow a right-hand fence beside a drive to a handgate leading into Studham Lane. Turn right onto this road, then, shortly after a left-hand bend, turn left over a stile onto path ED15, following a sporadic left-hand hedge to the A4146 at Dagnall.

Turn right onto this road, passing the 'Golden Rule'. Just past Cross Keys Farm on the left, turn left through a gate onto path ED18, passing the corner of a fence and bearing slightly left to a gate at the left-hand end of a hedge leading to a farmyard. Here go straight on past some farm buildings. Near the back of the farm bear left onto a track, passing a building with a wooden tower numbered '8'. Follow it, bearing slightly right out of the farm and through a hedge gap, then beside a left-hand hedge. Where the track turns right, leave it and bear slightly right across the field to its far corner. Here bear slightly left onto Hertfordshire bridleway LG1, crossing the next field to the corner of a hedge. Now bear left of the hedge and follow it to a farm track. Turn right onto this (soon on bridleway ED12a), heading towards Well Farm until you reach a left-hand hedge gap. Turn left through this, keeping left of a fence and swinging right beside a right-hand hedge (soon on LG1 again). Where the hedge ends, go straight on across a field to a bridlegate. Go through this gate, then bear slightly left across a field to a bridlegate into Hoo Wood.

Inside the wood, follow the obvious bridleway straight on uphill, ignoring all crossing tracks until, after more than a third of a mile, you reach a bridlegate into a field. Here follow the right-hand hedge straight on across the field to a gate and bridlegate. Go through the bridlegate and turn right onto LG19, following a right-hand hedge to a gate and kissing-gate onto a road at Little Gaddesden. Do not go through these, but turn sharp left onto path LG18 doubling back across the field to cross two stiles, then bear half right across the next field to the corner of a fence by a tall oak tree. Follow this right-hand fence straight on to a kissing-gate, from which the fifteenth-century church comes into view ahead.

This church is principally notable for the wealth of memorials which it contains to members of the Egerton family, the Earls and Dukes of Bridgewater, who held nearby Ashridge Park from 1604 to 1849, including one to the third and last Duke who inspired the construction of the Grand Union Canal and is consequently known as 'The Father of British Inland Navigation'.

Now go straight on across a field to pass through two kissing-gates and reach Church Road, then follow this straight on past the church to a stile opposite the second gate into the churchyard. Turn right over this, then immediately left onto path LG14, following a left-hand fence to cross a stile. Now bear slightly left across a field to a concealed stile in the hedge ahead. Cross this and follow a left-hand hedge straight on for a third of a mile to a stile near an oak tree, where you meet but do not join the route of Walk 13. Do **not** cross this stile, but instead, joining the Chiltern Way, turn left through a hedge gap onto path LG12 and follow a right-hand hedge downhill through two fields (later on bridleway LG11, then ST33) to reach the A4146 in the Gade valley above the source of its river.

Cross this main road, go through a gap by a gate opposite and take bridleway ST25 following a left-hand hedge uphill. Soon after the hedge bears right, go through the second gap in it and continue uphill

WALK 17

95

between a deer fence protecting a young plantation and a belt of trees with fine views to your left towards Ivinghoe Beacon to reach a gate into Ravensdell Wood. Go through this and follow a track through the wood to another gate, then follow a right-hand hedge for a few yards to a stile in it. Turn right over this onto path ST26, then bear half left across a large field, heading towards some distant houses on the edge of Studham to reach a stile. Cross this and bear slightly right across the next field to a stile and gate left of a large red-brick house leading into a lane. Follow this lane out to Common Road and cross this, bearing half right to a hedge gap. Go through this and leaving the Chiltern Way, take path ST16, bearing half right across a field following what is normally a crop break to the right-hand corner of a large house ahead which was formerly the village school. Here bear right through a gap onto Studham Common, following bridleway ST17 along the valley bottom, then through a belt of scrub. On emerging onto open common by a football pitch, bear left to meet Church Road opposite the Methodist Church, then turn right onto this road for your starting point.

WALK 18: Whipsnade Downs

Length of Walk: (A) 6.8 miles / 10.9 Km
(B) 2.5 miles / 4.0 Km

Starting Point: Whipsnade Downs National Trust car park.

Grid Ref: TL000184

Maps: OS Landranger Sheet 166
OS Explorer Sheet 182
OS Pathfinder Sheet 1095 (TL01/11)
Chiltern Society FP Map No. 21

How to get there / Parking: Whipsnade Downs, 2.5 miles southwest of Dunstable, may be reached from the town by taking the B489 towards Aston Clinton for 2.5 miles to the 'Plough Inn' roundabout. Here turn left onto the B4506 towards Dagnall, then, after a quarter mile, turn left again onto the B4540 up Whipsnade Downs. Near the top, look out for the signposted Whipsnade Downs Car Park on your left.

Notes: Deep mud may be encountered on bridleway WP1 even in dry weather, as may heavy nettle growth in the summer months.

Whipsnade Downs and nearby Dunstable Downs both provide a rural playground for nearby built-up areas, the lofty location of which offers panoramic views over the Ouzel valley and beyond, as well as a pleasant breeze even on the hottest day. The nearby village of Whipsnade, which is visited by both walks, is notable for the extensive green around which its scattered cottages are situated and being the highest village in Bedfordshire. Its brick-built church has a sixteenth-century tower and eighteenth-century nave but incorporates some details of an earlier building, while at the back of the village is the Tree Cathedral planted in the 1930s by E.K.Blyth in memory of friends killed in the First World War and now looked after by the National Trust. However what Whipsnade is best known for is the Wild Animal Park which was opened by the Royal Zoological Society in 1931 to exhibit its hardier animals in natural surroundings. The Wild Animal Park in its scenically spectacular setting can be toured by a steam railway which you may hear in the course of your walk.

WALK 18

98

Both walks commence by taking you along the crest of the Downs with superb views before making for Whipsnade village, while Walk A additionally explores the upland plateau around Studham with its pleasant mixture of woods and farmland.

Starting from Whipsnade Downs Car Park, **both walks** climb a flight of steps on its east side, then turn left onto a National Trust permissive path, keeping left at a fork, ignoring a crossing bridleway and soon emerging through a gate onto open downland. Now follow a right-hand hedge later a fence straight on, wiggling to your right at one point, with panoramic views to your left including Ivinghoe Beacon, the prominent fourteenth-century Edlesborough Church on its hillock, Totternhoe Knolls, the site of a Bronze Age fort and Norman castle and later Dunstable Downs ahead. After half a mile, at the far end of Sallowspring Wood to your right, turn right following the fence of the wood to a bridlegate in the field corner. Go through this and briefly joining the Chiltern Way, take fenced bridleway WP1 straight on along the edge of the wood, soon crossing a macadam drive and continuing beside the wood, now with a hedge to your left. On approaching a track in woodland to your right, do **not** join it but, leaving the Chiltern Way, bear slightly left into a sunken way, still following the edge of the wood, then passing through it. Now keep straight on along the edge of a field to a crossing track, then take a green lane straight on downhill, eventually ignoring a branching lane to your left and shortly emerging onto Whipsnade Green. Here follow a grassy track bearing right uphill to reach the B4540.

Having crossed the road, **Walk B** turns right and follows the B4540 verge to a sharp right-hand bend. Here cross a side-road and now read the last paragraph. For **Walk A** ignore a macadam drive to your left and take a grassy track straight on across the green to the churchyard gate. Here, briefly rejoining the Chiltern Way, take path WP8 into the churchyard, leaving the gravel path and passing right of the church then bearing half left to cross a stile in the back hedge. Follow a left-hand hedge to cross a stile by a gate, then, leaving the Chiltern Way, take path ST11 straight on beside a right-hand hedge. At the far end of the field cross a stile and turn left into Dunstable Road. On reaching a corner of Heath Wood to your right, turn right through a hedge gap onto path ST12 and follow the outside edge of the wood to the far side of the field. Here take a fenced path straight on between gardens to a road called Woodland Rise at Holywell.

Turn left onto its pavement and follow it round a bend. Just past house no. 25 turn left onto a fenced path (still ST12). Shortly before the far end of the left-hand fence, fork right onto a woodland path, soon passing the backs of a number of gardens and becoming ST37. After a quarter mile at a crossways take path ST4 straight on, soon bearing right and following the inside edge of the wood uphill, soon with a garden hedge to your right. On emerging into a field, follow a right-hand hedge straight on then at the far side of the field take a fenced path straight on along the outside edge of a wood. After some 70 yards turn left into the wood onto winding path ST13 which takes you straight across the wood ignoring two crossing paths. At the far side of the wood, go straight on across a field to the near right-hand corner of a copse called Ashen Grove. Follow its outside edge straight on to the far end of the copse, then go straight on across the field, passing right of a tree to reach the corner of a hedge. Now follow this hedge straight on to the back corner of a garden, then take a fenced path straight on beside the garden to a road at Byslips.

Turn right onto this road and follow it for over 200 yards passing Hill Farm. At a double bend turn right over a concealed stile onto path ST2 and bear slightly left across a field to the corner of a copse called Caps Grove. Here turn left and follow the edge of the copse to a stile, then bear slightly right across the next field to cross some rails by a gate at the corner of Bell Wood. Now go straight on through two paddocks and along a fenced path to Dunstable Road by the 'Bell'. Turn left onto this road then immediately right onto path ST1, keeping right of a concrete wall and following it, soon with a hedge to your right. Where the wall ends, take the fenced path straight on, soon passing through a copse. On entering a field, turn left and follow a left-hand hedge around two sides of the field, then turn left onto path ST3, a grassy track following a right-hand hedge. At the far side of the next field ignore a stile ahead and turn right onto path ST18 (joining Walk 17), then follow this grassy track beside a left-hand hedge. At the far side of the field take the track straight on through a hedge gap, then bearing half right (now on path ST19) to the corner of a tree-belt surrounding Studham churchyard. Here join a farm road bearing half left past the churchyard to reach a crossing track, then take path ST21 straight on over a stile, following a right-hand fence past two trees and then bearing slightly left and diverging from the fence to reach a stile and footbridge into a wood called Church Grove.

Cross these and (leaving Walk 17 and rejoining the Chiltern Way) turn right onto bridleway ST6 along the inside edge of the wood. Where this forks, go right, leaving the wood and taking a grassy track beside a right-hand hedge straight on through two fields to enter a copse. Here ignore a branching bridleway to the left and go straight on through the copse, then continue between the perimeter fence of Whipsnade Wild Animal Park and a thick hedge for a third of a mile to Studham Lane. Turn left onto this disused road and follow it straight on for nearly half a mile, ignoring a left-hand fork and a footpath to your right (where you leave the Chiltern Way) and emerging onto Whipsnade Green.

Just before the junction of Studham Lane and the B4540, fork left onto a worn path along the verge of the B4540 rejoining **Walk B**. **Walks A and B** now follow the B4540 verge to the beginning of a triangular green on the other side of the road. Here cross the road and take a worn path across the rear of the green to join a macadam access road. Follow this straight on to its end, then go straight on through a bridlegate onto fenced bridleway WP6. After passing a bungalow, continue straight on, now climbing gently between hedges for a third of a mile to the top of Whipsnade Downs, where the bridleway (now EB17) begins to descend again and reaches open downland. Here bear half left to reach the steps leading down into the car park.

WALK 19:   Dunstable Downs

Length of Walk: 6.8 miles / 10.9 Km
Starting Point: Entrance to the main car park on
                    Dunstable Downs.
Grid Ref: TL008198
Maps: OS Landranger Sheets 165 & 166
        OS Explorer Sheets 192, 193 & 181 or 182
        OS Pathfinder Sheets 1071 (SP82/92), 1072 (TL02/12)
        & 1095 (TL01/11)
        (virtually all) Chiltern Society FP Map No. 21
How to get there / Parking: Dunstable Downs car park,
    1.5 miles south of the town centre, may be reached from it
    by taking the B489 towards Aston Clinton, then turning
    left onto the B4541 towards The Downs and Whipsnade.
    At the top of the hill, park in one of the right-hand car
    parks near a low building with a pointed roof (the
    Countryside Centre and toilet block).
Notes: Deep mud may be encountered on TT12, even in dry
    weather, while heavy nettle growth may also be found in
    summer, particularly on path TT23.

The Dunstable Downs, with their spectacular views along the
Chilterns to Ivinghoe Beacon and out across the Vale of
Aylesbury towards Oxfordshire and the Cotswolds, are today a
real 'honeypot' for people from Dunstable, Luton and farther
afield, for picnics and walks with superb views and convenient
parking. Four thousand years ago, these hills must also have
been frequented, as at the northern end of the Downs are the
Five Knolls, five huge Neolithic or Bronze Age burial barrows,
where excavations have not only revealed remains from this
period, but also a large number of skeletons originating from
the fifth century AD, some of whom had injured bones or their
hands tied behind their backs suggesting that they were the
victims of some battle or massacre.

Much of the walk, indeed, traverses terrain which has
yielded evidence of early settlement, as, after passing the Five
Knolls, you descend to the junction of the Ancient British
Icknield Way and the equally ancient Green Lane, before
following Green Lane past the Bronze Age camp known as

Maiden Bower and modern lime pits and continuing to Totternhoe with its Bronze Age hill fort, Norman castle earthworks and mediaeval stone pits at Lower End and the site of a Roman villa at Church End. In addition to its historical aspects, the walk also provides a series of fine views and visits places of flora and fauna interest and so has something to offer for everyone.

Starting from the entrance to the main macadamed car park on Dunstable Downs by the Countryside Centre and toilets, bear half right across the car park to a macadam path out of its rear right-hand corner. Where this path bears right towards the Countryside Centre, leave it and joining the Chiltern Way, take a mown grass path parallel to the B4541 straight on along the top of the ridge with fine views to your left towards Totternhoe Knolls and beyond. You soon pass through an overflow car park, then continue straight on to a gate and bridlegate right of a kissing-gate where you join a chalky path, also part of the Icknield Way long-distance path. Take this worn path straight on rounding a steep-sided combe called Pascomb Pit, where views across Dunstable open out to your right, taking the central option at a three-way fork and climbing to the summit at the end of the Downs with its superb panoramic views. Now take a permissive path straight on, descending gently past the Five Knolls to reach several gates. Here go through a kissing-gate and follow a worn path straight on downhill, joining path D23 to reach a mown green on the edge of Dunstable. Go straight on across the green heading for the left-hand side of a roundabout at the junction of the B489 and B4541.

At the roundabout, cross the B489 (Tring Road), then bear half right, passing through a gap beside a padlocked gate into the appropriately named Green Lane (D4). Now follow this tree-lined lane straight on for three-quarters of a mile, at first between housing estates, then (as TT12) leaving the town behind and ignoring a branching green lane to your left. On reaching a crossing green lane, leaving the Chiltern Way, take TT12, straight on for almost another half mile, passing within 150 yards of Maiden Bower hidden by the right-hand hedge. Where the lane turns left, leave it and take hedged path TT43 straight on, soon with the left-hand hedge giving way to a fence and views opening out across a restored lime pit to your left and towards Stanbridge ahead. After some 350 yards you leave the quarry behind and go straight on downhill through scrubland. Where the path eventually forks, go left (still on TT43), climbing a chalky slope to a stile, then turn left following a left-hand fence with views to your right towards Tilsworth and Stanbridge in places. On leaving the scrub behind, take a grassy track straight on towards Totternhoe

Limeworks, soon entering a sunken way and reaching a gate and stile into a green lane. Turn left into this lane (TT2) and follow it for some 250 yards. On nearing the limeworks, ignore a crossing track, then turn right into another green lane (TT45). After about 200 yards, at a junction of tracks, turn left onto byway TT24, a rough lane leading to the end of a macadam road at Totternhoe Lower End.

Take this road straight on to the limeworks gates. Here turn left onto fenced path TT23 to the right of the gates and drive, soon turning right, then left, then right again across fields to reach a squeeze-stile leading in a few yards to a green lane (TT1). Turn sharp left onto this, following it up Castle Hill. Some 50 yards before a sharp right-hand bend, turn right over a stile onto path TT28 leading into an undulating area called 'Little Hills' where Totternhoe stone, used amongst other things in the building of Windsor Castle, was excavated from the twelfth century onwards. To your left is the castle mound capped by the earthworks of a wooden Norman castle superimposed on a Bronze Age fort, while its use for defensive purposes by the Saxons is also indicated by the Saxon name of Totternhoe, which means 'look-out house hill'.

Here ignore a branching path to your right and bear slightly left across the undulating ground passing through a deep gully and a clump of bushes to reach a rise near the bottom of the castle mound where there are fine views out across the Ouzel valley into the Vale of Aylesbury, then bear slightly right for a stile into scrubland. Cross this and pass through the scrub into a beechwood, then bear left, ignoring a branching path to your right and following the contours of the hill until you reach a crossing path with steps (TT29). Turn right onto this, descending steeply, ignoring two branching paths to your left and eventually reaching a road at Totternhoe Middle End.

Cross this road and turn left along its pavement, passing the thatched, timber-framed 'Cross Keys'. At a left-hand bend, turn right onto path TT21 beside house no. 181, descending between fences into a small field. Now follow its left-hand fence straight on to a footbridge. Cross this and bear half left following a left-hand hedge to cross a stile. Now turn left over a stile by a gate onto path TT19 following a left-hand hedge and stream through two fields. At the far side of the second field, cross a culvert in a hedge gap and follow a left-hand hedge and stream to a field corner. Here bear right ignoring a footbridge to your left and follow a left-hand hedge to a footbridge and stile near a tall tree. Turn left over these and go straight on across a field to a footbridge left of gates ahead, then follow a right-hand hedge straight on. Soon after the hedge ends, turn right over a stile onto path TT20, then bear left across two fields, heading for a building with a small turret and weather vane and crossing a stile at one point, to

WALK 19

DUNSTABLE

SEWELL

'Pheasant Inn'

B 489

B 4541

Chiltern Way

Five Knolls

Pascomb Pit

Chiltern Way

Ichnield Way

Greenl Lane and Chiltern Way

Maiden Bower

Chalk Pit

TT 12

TT 12

TT 43

Lime Pit

TOTTERNHOE

CHURCH END

'Old Fam Inn'

Site of Roman Villa

TT 9

TT 20

TT 19

Doolittle Mill

TT 6

Gliding Club

B489

TT 7

TT 40

KN 10 / KN 18
Walk 20

Start

Dunstable

Downs

MIDDLE END

LOWER END

Lime Works

Castle Hill

'Cross Keys'

TT 23

TT 29

TT 21

TT 19

TT 28

TT 7

TT 45

TT 24

TT 2

II 43

N

1 mile

1 kilometre

0

0

EATON BRAY

105

reach another stile. Cross this, then turn left into a lane at Church End and follow it to a T-junction near Totternhoe's fifteenth-century church built in the local stone.

Here turn right into Church Road passing the church. Just after the pavement ends, by a macadam drive, cross the road and a stile opposite onto path TT9, bearing half right across a field to a stile. In this field, the site of a fourth-century Roman courtyard villa is to your left and there are fine views of the Dunstable Downs ahead. Now go straight on across the next field to a stile and footbridge midway between two clumps of trees, then bear slightly right across a further field to a stile at the corner of a fenceline leading to a bend in a road. Take this road straight on looking out for the remains of a disused wind- and watermill called Doolittle Mill partially hidden by trees ahead. At a right-hand bend just before the mill, turn left onto bridleway TT6, following a track beside a right-hand belt of trees for over half a mile to reach Wellhead Road.

Turn right onto this and at a road junction, cross the B489 and take bridleway TT7, a green lane, straight on towards the Downs. At the foot of the Downs go through a bridlegate, then turn right onto path TT40 following a right-hand fence over a rise into the next dip. Here, just before reaching a bridlegate and kissing-gate ahead, turn left onto a permissive path following a right-hand fence steeply uphill. Half-way up the hill, stop for a rest and turn round for a view across the gliding club airstrip towards Totternhoe, then continue uphill to gates leading to the open hilltop with the visitor centre and toilets and your starting point straight ahead.

WALK 20:   Dunstable

Length of Walk: 7.6 miles / 12.2 Km

Starting Point: Salvation Army chapel at junction of
                      Icknield Street, Bullpond Lane and
                      Burr Street, Dunstable.

Grid Ref: TL017216

Maps: OS Landranger Sheet 166
           OS Explorer Sheets 182 & 193
           OS Pathfinder Sheets 1072 (TL02/12) & 1095 (TL01/11)
           Chiltern Society FP Map No. 21

How to get there / Parking: From the junction of the A5,
   A505 and B489 in the centre of Dunstable take the B489
   (West Street) towards Aston Clinton, then take the second
   turning left (Icknield Street) where a car park is on your
   left.

Notes: Paths D19 and D21 may be affected by the construction
   of the A5 (Dunstable Bypass).

Dunstable, at the crossroads of the prehistoric Icknield Way
and Watling Street, a Roman road from Dover via London to
Holyhead, is believed to have been inhabited since the Stone
Age as archaeologists have made finds dating from various
ages in close proximity to the town. Although a Roman staging
post known as Durocobrivae was recorded, it is believed not to
have been very large and it was only in 1131, when King Henry I
founded an Augustinian priory and constructed a royal lodge
known as Kingsbury, that 'Dunestaple' (as it was then known)
became a place of any size. Originally the Priory was of vast
proportions being 320 feet long and having transepts 150 feet
wide, but the west towers collapsed in a storm in 1222 and the
transepts, central tower, long choir and monastic buildings
were at some stage demolished to leave the present parish
church with its massive Norman columns, round arches and
fifteenth-century north tower. In 1533 the Priory was also the
scene of a major historical event as it was here that Thomas
Cranmer, the then Archbishop of Canterbury, pronounced the
annulment of the marriage of Henry VIII and Catherine of Aragon
which led to the English Reformation. In the eighteenth
century improved road communications caused Dunstable to

WALK 20

108

become an important port of call for stagecoaches and so the town's inns flourished, as did the local straw-hat industry, but it has only been in the last century that the town has mushroomed into the large industrial town it is today.

The walk, which explores the downland around Dunstable, for which the town is famous, first passes through the town centre before skirting the lofty ridge of Blow's Down, which, to some extent, still separates Dunstable from its larger neighbour Luton. It then leads you across the A5 in its valley to Kensworth Church End in a quiet Chiltern hollow before following a high ridge round Kensworth Quarry to reach the top of the Dunstable Downs. From here your return route traverses a downland golf course with superb views across the town before descending to your starting point.

Starting by the Salvation Army chapel at the junction of Icknield Street, Bullpond Lane and Burr Street, take Icknield Street to the B489 (West Street) (part of the Icknield Way), then turn right and follow it to its junction with the A5 (High Street) (part of Watling Street) and the A505. Here take the A505 (Church Street) straight on past the Book Castle, the parish church and the 'Old Palace Lodge' and 'Norman King' on the site of the royal lodge of Kingsbury. At the far end of the churchyard turn right into Priory Road, then left into St. Peters Road. Disregard one turning to the right and at a second junction, fork right into Bigthan Road then fork immediately left into a fenced alleyway which leads you to a road junction.

Here cross the major road bearing slightly right and taking path D19 virtually opposite. Where this path forks, take the right-hand option straight on over a stile towards Blow's Down soon passing under a pylon where you ignore a crossing track. On reaching the end of a residential road called Half Moon Lane, take path D21 straight on through a kissing-gate, then keep right of the power lines. At the far end of a row of houses to your right, fork left onto a lesser path soon joining a grassy sunken track. Just before the far end of a line of bushes to your right, fork right to join another sunken way which keeps right of the power lines, then at a fork bear right again to pass right of the next pylon. Now the sunken way begins to climb passing under the power lines, with wide views across the town opening out to your right. Ignore a major crossing track and keep straight on, soon joining a left-hand fence then dropping again to a kissing-gate. Here take path CA11 straight on through scrub. After some 200 yards ignore a crossing path and go straight on through a hedge into a field. Now turn right and follow a right-hand hedge. After about 150 yards by a marker post, bear half left across the field to a corner of Dame Ellen's Wood, then follow its outside edge straight on to meet a farm road. Turn right onto this (soon on path CA12) and follow its winding course for half a mile to reach Dunstable Road.

Turn left onto its left-hand pavement and follow it round a long right-hand bend. Where the pavement ends, cross the road and continue along its verge to a left-hand bend. Here turn right over a stile onto path CA14 following a left-hand hedge to the far end of the field, then a right-hand hedge straight on downhill to a stile onto the A5 opposite Lodge Farm.

Cross this road and turn left along it. After some 50 yards turn right just before metal gates onto path KN3 passing an industrial site to enter a field. Here follow the right-hand hedge straight on uphill to a small gate into a belt of trees then turn right onto a track in the tree belt. After about 60 yards, on reaching a crossing track, turn left, *not* joining the track but passing through a hedge gap left of it. Now follow a right-hand hedge uphill and down again. At the bottom of the dip go through a gap in the right-hand hedge and follow the other side of the hedge straight on uphill. At the top of the rise where the hedge turns left, bear right onto path KN6 crossing the field heading just right of Kensworth Church and left of a twin-poled electricity pylon to reach a grassy track leading to Beech Road. Cross this road and take the drive to Bury Farm straight on. On reaching the farm, at a three-way fork bear right following a left-hand hedge and line of trees bordering the churchyard.

By a stile into the churchyard of this church dating from around 1120, turn right onto path KN4, joining a left-hand hedge by an oak tree at the top of a rise. Now, by a tall ash tree, turn left onto path KN19 following a short green lane along the edge of a wood. On reaching a crossing track, turn right onto path KN7, still following the edge of the wood over a rise where Kensworth Quarry comes into view to your left. Now ignore a branching path to your right and in the valley bottom bear half left, still following the edge of the wood, soon with the quarry fence enclosing the track to your left. From here you follow the quarry fence for three-quarters of a mile, ignoring another branching path to your right, soon with superb views to your right across Dunstable to Blow's Down and several ranges of hills beyond. Having passed through a kissing-gate, continue to follow the quarry fence to a signposted junction. Here turn right up a steep bank and follow the edge of a left-hand wood, soon with a superb view across Dunstable opening out ahead. Where the edge of the wood turns left, leave it and bear half left across open grassland to another corner of the wood where you fork left onto path D27 following the edge of the wood downhill to a corner. Here turn left onto path D28 entering the woodland. After about 250 yards turn right at a fork onto waymarked path KN18 and follow its winding course through the woods for half a mile ignoring all branching and crossing paths. At a T-junction turn right onto a crossing path at one point bearing left, then later passing through a squeeze-stile by a gate and eventually reaching the B4541 opposite the Dunstable Downs car park (the starting point of Walk 19).

If wishing to admire the panoramic views available from the Downs or use the public conveniences, cross the road; otherwise do *not* join it, but turn sharp right onto fenced path KN10 which leads you through a belt of scrub onto a golf course. Here take a grassy track straight on beside a line of trees with wide views ahead. On reaching the golf course car park, follow the yellow lines marking the path across it. At the far side take a visible path straight on, aiming for the end of a hedge ahead. Here pass between the hedge and a clump of hawthorn bushes to enter a hedged path. Take this straight on downhill, with the left-hand hedge giving way to an overgrown downland field at one point, before you pass through a belt of scrub to reach a squeeze-stile leading to a narrow macadam lane. Take this lane straight on downhill to join a residential road called Canesworde Road at a bend, then follow this straight on for a third of a mile ignoring all branching roads. Where it finally bears left and becomes Kirby Road, turn right through green gates into a recreation ground and follow a macadam path across it to gates on the far side. Go through these then turn left into Bullpond Lane to reach your starting point.

WALK 21:   Toddington

Length of Walk: (A)   11.1 miles / 17.8 Km
                        (B)   5.5 miles / 8.8 Km
Starting Point: 'Bell', Toddington.
Grid Ref: TL009289
Maps: OS Landranger Sheet 166
            OS Explorer Sheet 193
            OS Pathfinder Sheet 1072 (TL02/12)

How to get there / Parking: Toddington, 4.5 miles north
of Dunstable, may be reached by leaving the M1 at
Junction 12 (Toddington) and taking the A5120 towards
Toddington and Dunstable. On reaching the village green
known as Market Square, turn left and park around the
green. If there are no spaces available, take Leighton
Road (signposted to Tebworth) opposite and park along it
or in one of its side-streets.

Notes: Heavy nettle growth may be encountered in places in
summer, particularly on bridleway HA21 and paths SL4
and TD42.

Today Toddington is probably best known for its M1 service
area, but the village on its hilltop little more than a mile away
with its church, pubs and cottages ranged around a
picturesque green seems like a different world. In the past
Toddington would seem to have been a place of some
importance as it has an old town hall and its green is known as
Market Square recalling the fact that it was once a market
town. Its cruciform thirteenth-century church was lavishly
renovated and extended in the fifteenth century when the
wool trade had made the town rich. Inside this church is the
Wentworth Chapel where Henrietta Maria Wentworth was
buried in 1686. Born at Toddington in 1657, she became
mistress of the Duke of Monmouth, first natural son of
Charles II, who unsuccessfully attempted to overthrow
James II in 1685 and was subsequently executed. Just to the
east of the church is Conger Hill, a twelfth-century flat-topped
castle motte which provides superb views across the Flit
valley to a part of the Chiltern escarpment known as the

Barton Hills. The name 'Conger' is believed to be a corruption of 'conynger' meaning a 'rabbit warren'.

Both walks commence by crossing the village green and passing Conger Hill before traversing the Flit valley with wide views and climbing the Chiltern escarpment to Upper Sundon. Walk A then explores the quiet rolling hills to the north of Luton and visits Streatley (pronounced 'Strettley') before descending the escarpment, rejoining Walk B and returning to Toddington.

Both walks start by the 'Bell' in Toddington, crossing the A5120, passing the church and the 'Oddfellows Arms' and entering Conger Lane. Just past some thatched cottages to your left turn left through a kissing-gate and fork half right onto path TD42 across the field, passing just right of the castle mound known as Conger Hill and its moat, then bearing slightly left to a gate and kissing-gate in the far corner of the field. Go through the kissing-gate and take bridleway TD43, a fenced track past a cemetery with fine views of the Barton Hills ahead. Now ignore a branching track to your left and take a grassy track straight on across fields. Where the left-hand side of the track becomes a ditch, keep right of it and follow it. Where the ditch bears left, leave it and take footpath TD43 straight on across a field heading for a single pylon right of a double-pole pylon to reach a fence gap onto the B530.

Cross this road and turn right along its far verge, almost immediately turning left over a stile onto path TD45, heading for the left-hand corner of the sewage works ahead. Here take path TD47 straight on towards the near left-hand corner of Woodcock Wood to cross a footbridge over the River Flit, then keep straight on to the corner of the wood. Now turn left over the footbridge, then turn right and follow the outside edge of the wood uphill. At the top corner of the wood follow a line of trees straight on across the field to the right-hand end of Hipsey Spinney. Go straight on past this wood, then continue to a hedge gap ahead where you cross a stile and culvert. Now bear slightly right heading for the right-hand of two hills ahead to reach the near corner of a wiggle in the hedge flanking the M1. Here go through a fence gap and take a path through scrubland to another fence gap leading to a bridge over the M1. Turn left over this bridge then follow a concrete farm road. Where the concrete ends, bear slightly left to cross a railway footbridge, then take path SU2, a sunken lane, straight on uphill. On reaching a macadam road, follow it straight on uphill between old overgrown chalk quarries for over a third of a mile. After the road levels out, where it bears right, leave it, going straight on between bollards into a narrow macadam lane which soon becomes a village street at Upper Sundon. At a T-junction by the 'Crown', bear slightly left into Harlington Road and follow it to the 'Red Lion'. Now **Walk A** omits the next paragraph.

Just past the 'Red Lion' **Walk B** turns left into bridleway SU3, a green lane, joining the Chiltern Way and eventually reaching gates into a field. Now follow a grassy track straight on. After some 350 yards, just before the gates of a sewage works, fork right through a bridlegate by a field gate and cross a field diagonally to a bridlegate just left of its far corner. Leaving the Chiltern Way, go through this and take the obvious bridleway downhill along the inside edge of scrubland for a quarter mile eventually emerging into a field with a fine view ahead towards Harlington village on its low hill. Here turn left onto bridleway HA21, a grassy track following the left-hand hedge turning right at a corner of the field. Where the track turns right, leave it and follow the left-hand hedge straight on, rejoining **Walk A**. Now omit the next six paragraphs.

Just past the 'Red Lion', briefling joining the Chiltern Way, **Walk A** turns right onto path SU5 along the far edge of the green then between a pond and garden fences to a kissing-gate. Now go straight on across a playing field heading towards a tall pylon in the valley ahead to reach another kissing-gate. Now, leaving the Chiltern Way, go straight on to the end of a sporadic hedge, then turn left onto path SU14 along the near side of this hedge to reach a stile. Cross this, soon entering the 'White Hart' car park, and take its drive straight on out to Streatley Road. Turn right onto this road, then at a sharp left-hand bend, leave the road and take path SU11 following a right-hand hedge straight on for a third of a mile to Manor Road on the edge of Lower Sundon. Although having only a couple of farms and a few cottages, Lower Sundon can boast a large thirteenth-century church with mediaeval wall paintings and stone seats around its walls for the infirm from the time before pews were provided. In the seventeenth century this church was the scene of the wedding between William Foster, a persecutor of the non-conformist preacher John Bunyan, and Anne Wingate, sister of the magistrate who had Bunyan imprisoned at Bedford Gaol.

Turn right onto this road, then after some 30 yards, turn left through a hedge gap onto path SU12 to reach a junction of farm roads. Here take a farm road straight on for a third of a mile, soon passing Sundon Wood. At the far side of the wood, where the farm road turns left, bear slightly right, soon joining and following the left side of a hedge, with views of Galley Hill, Warden Hill and part of Luton opening out ahead. On reaching a waymarking post, bear half left across the field, heading towards a pylon in the next field to reach a gap in the bottom hedge where you cross a footbridge onto path SL5.

Now turn left and follow a left-hand hedge for three-quarters of a mile, at one point turning right and then left and eventually climbing to reach a wiggle in the hedge near George Wood. Here bear half right across the field to join and follow the left side of a winding sporadic tree belt, now with closer views of Galley Hill and Warden Hill to your left. On reaching a crossing fence, turn left and follow it, later a hedge past a modern hospice.

Where the hedge and fence bear right, turn left onto path SL4 across the field to the corner of a hedge just right of a pylon. Keep left of this hedge and follow it to a corner of George Wood, then go through a gap and follow a left-hand hedge through four fields. At the far end of the fourth field, cross a stile and bear half right across a field heading just left of a thatched cottage at Streatley to cross a stile just right of the end of a hedge. Here bear slightly left across the next field to cross a stile at the far side, then continue through scrubland to Sharpenhoe Road at Streatley.

Joining the Chiltern Way, turn left onto this road, then immediately left again into Bury Lane (path SL11). Take this lane past some cottages to a gate and stile then continue to a second gate. Here turn right over a stile by a gate and follow a grassy track uphill beside a right-hand hedge. Where the track turns right into Middle Farm, leave it and take a grassy path straight on to a stile into an alleyway. On reaching the end of a cul-de-sac road, cross it and take an alleyway straight on to a gate into Streatley churchyard. The fourteenth-century church with its fifteenth-century tower has a thirteenth-century font and a mediaeval wall painting of St. Catherine. In ruins for half a century, the church was thoroughly restored by Sir Albert Richardson in 1938.

Do not go through the churchyard gate, but, leaving the Chiltern Way, turn left into another alleyway (path SL12) to Sundon Road, then turn right onto its narrow pavement. At a road junction, fork left onto the left-hand pavement of Sharpenhoe Road, then at the far end of the houses, turn left down some steps onto enclosed path SL13. By the gates to a radio station, go straight on through a squeeze-stile into a field and follow its right-hand hedge. After some 200 yards turn right through a hedge gap and take fenced path SU15 to enter a wood at the far side of the field, where you join the reverse direction of Walk 22.

In the wood, rejoining the Chiltern Way, turn left onto path SL15 skirting the top of the escarpment with views through the trees to your right. Where the path forks, keep left. On reaching a waymarked crossways, leaving the Chiltern Way, turn left then immediately right through a fence gap onto path SU10 leaving the wood and bearing half-right across the corner of a field to cross a ladder-stile back into the wood. Here bear slightly right, ignoring a more distinct crossing path and continuing downhill. On leaving the wood where fine views open out ahead towards Harlington and Ampthill beyond, take path HA6 straight on downhill through scrub to a stile. Cross this and bear half left across a field to the left-hand end of a line of trees. Here go straight on through a hedge gap joining a farm track (bridleway HA27) and continuing along it for a quarter mile to reach a road. Leaving Walk 22 again, turn left onto this road, then at a road junction turn right and almost immediately left onto bridleway HA21 following a grassy track beside a left-hand hedge. After a third of a mile go through a hedge gap, then turn right beside the edge of a plantation then wasteland by farm buildings to your right. At a T-junction of tracks, turn left and follow a track to reach a hedge ahead where you turn right and rejoin **Walk B**.

Walks A and B now follow the hedge, soon turning right, then left then immediately left again over a bridge and follow a winding hedged bridleway for a quarter mile. On emerging into a field near a bridge under the railway, bear half left onto bridleway SU22 passing under this bridge, then turn right onto bridleway TD96 to reach a pylon. Here turn left through a hedge gap and bear slightly left across a field to a pylon in the middle of the field, then go straight on heading for a barn at Mill Farm beyond the M1. On joining a farm track at a bend, follow its winding course (soon on path TD55) for a quarter mile to Old Park Farm. Here, at a junction of tracks, turn left onto path TD54 keeping left of the buildings. Then bearing right, soon joining and bearing left onto a macadam drive, follow this over the River Flit and the M1. At the far side of the motorway, ignore a branching road to the left, then after about 70 yards turn left onto a rough track through a hedge gap into a field. Follow the right-hand hedge straight on for some 200 yards then turn right over a footbridge and two stiles and go straight across a field to a stile and footbridge by a gate in the corner of the field leading to the B530. Cross this road and take path TD42 straight on over a stile by a gate following a right-hand hedge to cross a stile. Now take the fenced path straight on uphill with views opening out to your left. On crossing another stile, follow the right-hand fence straight on, ignoring gates to your right, to reach a stile and footbridge into a copse. Go straight on through this, crossing another footbridge. On emerging into a field, turn right onto bridleway TD38 following a right-hand hedge then a fence to a field corner. Here go through a fence gap and turn left onto the continuation of path TD42, a fenced path along the edge of a cemetery. At the far end of the cemetery turn right onto fenced bridleway TD43 and retrace your steps into Toddington.

WALK 21

HARLINGTON

STREATLEY

LUTON

A 6

TODDINGTON

Start 'Bell'

A 5120

B 530

M 1

Jct.12

A 520

UPPER SUNDON

LOWER SUNDON

1 mile

1 kilometre

117

WALK 22: Harlington (Beds.)

Length of Walk: 6.0 miles / 9.7 Km
Starting Point: Harlington Village Hall car park.
Grid Ref: TL037304
Maps: OS Landranger Sheet 166
OS Explorer Sheet 193
OS Pathfinder Sheets 1048 (TL03/13) &
1072 (TL02/12)

How to get there / Parking: Harlington, 5.5 miles north
of Dunstable, may be reached by leaving the M1 at
Junction 12 (Toddington) and taking the A5120 towards
Ampthill. After half a mile turn right onto a road
signposted to Harlington Station and follow it to a
crossroads in the village. Here turn right into Sundon
Road where there is a car park by the village hall on
your left.

Harlington, on a gault foothill of the Chilterns capped by its
prominent thirteenth-century church, both catches the eye
when looking out from the escarpment and provides fine
views back towards the escarpment. Although the village with
its station and close proximity to an M1 junction, has
expanded considerably in recent years, this largely goes
unnoticed when looking from the Chilterns as most of the new
development is on the far side of the hill. In addition to its
church, Harlington can also boast a number of attractive
timber-framed and thatched cottages, but possibly its greatest
claim to fame is its seventeenth-century manor house,
one-time home of the magistrate Francis Wingate, who had the
non-conformist preacher John Bunyan arrested at nearby
Lower Samshill and brought to his house in Harlington, where
he was imprisoned for the night and tried before being sent to
Bedford Gaol where he wrote his 'Pilgrim's Progress'.

The walk, to which the view from the village positively
invites you, takes you from Harlington across the valley and
up the Chiltern escarpment near Streatley before leading you
onto the outcrop of Sharpenhoe Clappers, with its superb
views along the escarpment and out into the lowlands,
descending to Sharpenhoe village and returning to Harlington.

Starting from the car park by Harlington Village Hall opposite the 'Carpenters Arms', turn right onto Sundon Road. At the village crossroads, turn right into Church Road, then at a bend by the church, fork right onto macadam path HA27 across the recreation ground. On joining Barton Road, turn right and after some 40 yards turn right again through a hedge gap onto path HA6 following the outside edge of a copse with fine views of the escarpment ahead. Where the copse ends, take a winding crop-break generally straight on, keeping left of a ditch when it commences, then ignoring a bridge over it. On reaching the end of a hedge, cross the ditch and continue ahead until you reach a footbridge in front of you. Cross this and then head for a gap in trees on the skyline until you reach a field boundary. Here bear half left, keeping right of a hedge and following it to a footbridge leading to a road.

Turn right onto this road, then after a quarter mile at a right-hand bend, turn left through gates onto bridleway HA27 joining the reverse direction of Walk 21 and following a winding track. On joining a right-hand hedge, turn right through a hedge gap, then bear half left onto path HA6 crossing a large field to a stile into scrubland at the top of the second rise to your left. Cross this stile and a crossing path and follow path HA6 steeply uphill through scrub to an area of open downland where a seat gives you an opportunity to rest and admire the view across the lowlands behind you towards Harlington and Ampthill.

Now take path SU10 straight on uphill into mature beechwoods. At the far side of the wood, ignore a crossing path and go straight on over a ladder-stile into a field. Now bear half left across the field corner to a fence gap leading back into the wood. Just inside the wood turn left onto the Chiltern Way, then immediately right by a marker post at the top of some steps onto path SL15 and follow it straight on for 350 yards, ignoring branching paths to left and right and soon skirting the top edge of a deep coombe. At a waymarked fork where gates can be seen to your right, keep straight on, following the rim of the coombe, gradually bearing left and eventually crossing a stile, where there is a fine view ahead towards Harlington. Now bear slightly right, soon crossing a second stile, where fine views open out to your left towards Harlington, Sharpenhoe and Pulloxhill in the foreground and Ampthill beyond. Now go straight across the field to a stile and steps down to Sharpenhoe Road.

Cross this and take path SL14 straight on through a car park and a gap by a gate, then along a macadamed track. On passing through a gap by another gate, take a stone track along the edge of the scrub, gradually bearing left. By a marker post, leaving the Icknield Way long-distance path, keep left, entering the scrub, then, on emerging from the scrub, where a superb view opens out to your left towards Toddington, Harlington and Sharpenhoe, go straight on to reach the near left-hand corner of the mature beech copse within the ancient earthworks on Sharpenhoe Clappers known as Clappers Wood.

The name Sharpenhoe Clappers is of mixed origin, as the village name of Sharpenhoe is Saxon, meaning 'sharp spur of land', while Clappers comes from Norman French meaning 'rabbit warren'. While the village at the foot of the hill may therefore have originated in Saxon times, the hill shows much earlier signs of habitation, as it is capped by an Iron Age hill fort and both Iron Age and Roman pottery have been found there, but the Normans adapted it for breeding rabbits and thus arose the second part of its name. Clappers Wood within the earthworks, though ancient in appearance, was, in fact, only planted between 1834 and 1844 and a painting from 1815 shows it completely bare. In the wood is an obelisk erected by W. A. Robertson in memory of his two brothers who were killed in the First World War and this was also his reason for donating the Clappers to the National Trust in 1939.

Now continue between a fence and the earthwork to the far end of Clappers Wood. Here at a fork keep left leaving the Chiltern Way and take a flight of steps down the steep hill. At the bottom cross a stile and follow a left-hand hedge straight on to reach a road. Turn left onto this and follow it into Sharpenhoe village.

Sharpenhoe, at the foot of the Clappers, has always been a hamlet of the hilltop village of Streatley. Apart from sharing its name with the hill from which it derives, Sharpenhoe's other claim to fame is linked to the former moated manor, of which only the moat survives just to the east of Bury Farm. This house was home to both the sixteenth-century playwright Thomas Norton, a forerunner of and a model for Shakespeare and Marlowe, who was buried at Streatley in 1584 and the leading seventeenth-century mathematician, Edmund Wingate.

At a road junction by 'The Lynmore', turn right onto bridleway SL19, the drive to Bury Farm. Just past a left-hand house, wiggle slightly to your right and continue through a farmyard, passing left of some large barns onto a wide field track. After a third of a mile, on reaching a crossing power-line, turn left under the power-line onto bridleway SL18, crossing a bridlebridge and then following a left-hand ditch and the edge of a wood called Sharpenhoe Grove. At the far end of the wood, go straight on across the field, heading for a large house called Grange Farm to reach a gap in the next hedge. Now go straight on, aiming for the tallest tree left of Grange Farm to reach a hedge gap onto Harlington Road.

Turn right onto this road, then after a few yards, turn left through a hedge gap onto path SL16 and follow a right-hand hedge to the far end

WALK 22

HARLINGTON

SHARPENHOE

STREATLEY

Station

Start

'Old Sun'

'Carpenters Arms'

HA27

HA 6

HA18

Lower East End Farm

Willow Farm

HA 18

HA 6

HA 5

SL16

HA27

Walk 21

HA6

SU 10

Chiltern Way

SL 15

SL 15

Walk 21

Sharpenhoe Road

Chiltern Way

Sharpenhoe Clappers

Chiltern Way

SL14

SL14

SL19

Moat

Bury Farm

SL 18

Sharpenhoe Grove

Harlington Road

Grange Farm

SL 16

Harlington Mill

Lynmore

1 mile

1 kilometre

0

0

121

of the field. Now follow the brook to the left for a few yards, then by a small ash tree, ignore a large bridge over the brook to your right and cross a sleeper footbridge by the tree into the next field. Here continue to follow the right-hand hedge, wiggling to your right at one point, until you reach a footbridge in the hedge. Turn right across this onto path HA5. Now turn left and follow a left-hand ditch, ignoring a footbridge across it and soon turning right. At the far end of the field, go straight on through a hedge gap and over a footbridge to reach a road.

Cross this road, pass left of the gates opposite and cross a culvert onto path HA18, then turn right and follow a right-hand ditch and hedge. At a corner of the field, go straight on through a hedge gap, then turn left and follow a left-hand hedge. Where the hedge ends, turn right onto path HA6 (temporarily rejoining your outward route) following a ditch until you reach a footbridge across it. Cross this and take path HA18 bearing half right across the field to a group of trees right of some houses on the skyline and left of the field corner. By these trees enter a hedged path past back gardens leading to Sundon Road. Turn right onto this passing the 'Old Sun' to reach your starting point.

WALK 23: Barton-le-Clay

Length of Walk:	6.8 miles / 11.0 Km
Starting Point:	Barton-le-Clay Church.
Grid Ref:	TL085304

Maps: OS Landranger Sheet 166
OS Explorer Sheet 193
OS Pathfinder Sheets 1048 (TL03/13) & 1072 (TL02/12)

How to get there / Parking: Barton-le-Clay, 6 miles north of Luton, may be reached from the town by taking the A6 towards Bedford. After about 5 miles, fork left onto the B655 towards Hitchin. On reaching the village, turn right, (still on the B655), then, at the second sharp left-hand bend, turn right into Church Road and find a suitable parking space.

Barton-le-Clay, formerly known as Barton-in-the-Clay, sits astride the old route of the A6 from London to Bedford and the Northwest of England at the foot of the Chiltern escarpment and as such, in the days of the stagecoach, was a place of busy coaching inns. Despite the village being swamped by modern housing in the 1960s and 1970s, the vicinity of its thirteenth-century church with its fifteenth-century tower and finely-carved roof depicting eagles, saints and apostles, its moated sixteenth-century rectory and a number of attractive cottages, remains an area of rural tranquillity and beauty. For the walker, however, Barton's principal attraction is as a centre for walks with spectacular views of and from the range of hills which bears its name and represents the northern-most ridge in the Chilterns and which are thought to have been the inspiration for John Bunyan's 'delectable mountains' in 'Pilgrim's Progress'.

The walk, indeed, first takes you from Barton through arable fields below the escarpment, offering fine views of the hills, to the Hertfordshire village of Hexton, before climbing up a wooded combe to explore the hilltop plateau near the Icknield Way to the south. It then culminates by emerging at the top of a spectacular downland combe which it skirts before descending gently back into Barton.

WALK 23

B 655

BARTON-LE-CLAY

'Royal Oak'

'Coach & Horses'

BC23

BC2

B 655

BC 23   SH 57

HX 6

HX5 Manor Farm

Walk 25

'Raven'

HEXTON

Church Wood

Hexton Manor

B 655

Rectory Farm

Start

BC 26

HX 2

Barton Hills

BC 26

BC16

Ravensburgh Castle

Lion Hill

Leet Wood

Barton Springs

BC 19

BC 1

BC 16

Stonley Wood

N

Barton Hill Farm

BC 16

SL 41

HX 2

HX 1

Mortgrove Farm

Walk 24

HX8/LL23   Way

Icknield

Maulden Firs

SL 41

SL 23

Walk 24

0   1mile

0   1kilometre

124

Starting from the entrance to Barton-le-Clay Church, take Church Road back to the B655. Here turn right, then immediately left into Manor Road, formerly known by the intriguing name of Rogues Lane. After a third of a mile, just past house no. 113 ('Oakengates'), turn right between safety barriers onto path BC2. Take this enclosed macadam path to a footbridge, then turn left with fine views of the hills to your right and follow a left-hand hedge to a field corner where you turn right. After about 70 yards, turn left through a hedge gap, then turn right onto path BC23 following a right-hand hedge straight on. Where the hedge ends, take a grassy track straight on with Shillington Church and a water tower at Upper Stondon coming into view on hilltops to your left. On reaching the end of a hedge, keep right of it, then, at its far end, follow the grassy track turning left then right. Now follow a right-hand hedge, eventually wiggling to the right, to reach a corner of the field. Here go straight on through a hedge gap and take path SH57 following a right-hand hedge to a footbridge into Hertfordshire at the far end of the field. Cross this, then bear half right onto path HX5, crossing the field diagonally to reach a road by the right-hand end of a row of bungalows at Hexton.

The village of Hexton, in a salient of Hertfordshire surrounded on three sides by Bedfordshire, has traditionally been an estate village. Before the First World War, it was almost completely rebuilt by the then Lord of the Manor, George Hodgson. Earlier owners of the Manor, Caroline Young and her French émigré husband, Joseph de Lautour, as well as adding two wings to the eighteenth-century Manor, built a new village school and village pump and also partially rebuilt the twelfth-century church. Two sides of its fifteenth-century tower, which was not rebuilt at this period, collapsed in 1947 and since then the tower has remained a ruin.

Turn right onto the road into the village and at a T-junction, turn right again following the village street past the 'Raven' and a high wall surrounding Hexton Manor to reach a crossroads by the ornate village pump. Here cross the B655 and take the Lilley road straight on. After some 200 yards, at a left-hand bend, fork right through a gate onto path HX2 and take this green lane straight on. Where its hedges end, follow the track straight on to a fork where you keep left and take a grassy track steeply uphill between woods. At the top of the hill, follow the grassy track straight on along the outside edge of the right-hand wood. At the far end of the field go straight on through a hedge gap, then turn right, still following the outside edge of the wood. After some 80 yards, at a corner of the field, turn left and follow the left side of a hedge for a third of a mile to a hedge gap ahead leading to a road. Turn right onto this road, then, just past the end of a tree belt, turn left through white gates onto bridleway HX1, the macadam drive to Mortgrove Farm. At the farm, follow the drive straight on past the buildings, then go straight on through a gap between gates and follow a right-hand fence, later a hedge, straight on for a quarter mile to the Icknield Way (HX8/LL23).

Turn right onto this Ancient British green road named after Boadicea's people, the Iceni, (joining the reverse direction of Walk 24) and follow it (later as SL41) for nearly half a mile towards Galley Hill, believed to be a corruption of 'Gallows Hill' as the remains of fifteenth-century gallows victims have been found in an older barrow there. Where a tree belt begins to your right, turn right onto a grassy track beside a right-hand hedge (leaving Walk 24 again) and follow it (still SL41) for two-thirds of a mile through two fields, with wide views to your left towards Luton and Streatley at the top of the first rise.

On reaching a road, turn left onto it, then, after about 150 yards, turn right onto bridleway BC16, a stony track beside a right-hand hedge. Where, after a quarter mile, the hedge ends, continue to follow the track bearing slightly left across a field with views towards lowland Bedfordshire opening out ahead. At the far side of the field, ignore a branching bridleway to your right and follow the track (now path BC1) straight on for about 30 yards, then turn right over a stile into scrubland onto path BC15 and immediately fork right onto path BC19, soon crossing another stile. Now follow a right-hand hedge straight on past the top of a steep combe, at the foot of which are Barton Springs. At the far end of the field, turn left and follow a right-hand fence to a gate and stile in it. Cross the stile and continue along a stony track on the other side of the fence (bridleway BC16 again), passing the top of another part of the combe and Ravensburgh Castle, a 22-acre Iron Age hill fort in woods half a mile to your right. At a fork, take bridleway BC26, a grassy track, straight on over the brow of the hill, then descending and swinging left round the face of the hill, at one point passing an old chalkpit. Where the track ends in a field, turn right and then bear left to follow a right-hand hedge, soon with a fence to your left, to reach the end of Church Road. Here turn right for your starting point.

WALK 24: Lilley (Treasures Grove Picnic Area)

Length of Walk: 7.4 miles / 11.9 Km

Starting Point: Northeast end of Treasures Grove Picnic Area on the Icknield Way north of Lilley.

Grid Ref: TL109283

Maps: OS Landranger Sheet 166
OS Explorer Sheet 193
OS Pathfinder Sheet 1072 (TL02/12)

How to get there / Parking: Treasures Grove Picnic Area, 4.5 miles north of Luton, may be reached from the town by taking the A505 towards Hitchin. 1 mile beyond the edge of the town, fork left onto a road signposted to Great Offley, Lilley and Kings Walden. At a T-junction, turn left onto the Lilley and Hexton road and follow this winding road for over 2 miles passing through Lilley and eventually reaching Treasures Grove Picnic Area in front of you at a sharp left-hand bend.

Treasures Grove Picnic Area, on the ancient Icknield Way near Lilley, might perhaps be expected to be a site where buried treasure had been found, but in fact it is named after an official of Hertfordshire County Council which created the picnic area. The village of Lilley, visited in the course of the walk, is clearly recognisable as an old estate village with a large number of its cottages bearing the lion rampant crest of the Docwra (pronounced 'Dockray') and later the Sowerby families of nearby Putteridge Bury. In the seventeenth century, Lilley was a centre of non-conformity being home to the religious writer, James Janeway, and it is believed that John Bunyan, author of 'Pilgrim's Progress', secretly preached in the cellar of one of the village cottages. An infamous later resident of the village was the nineteenth-century alchemist Johann Kellerman who disappeared from Lilley as suddenly as he came.

The walk, which includes a series of fine views, first leads you from Treasures Grove along the Icknield Way to near Telegraph Hill where a slight detour up the hill is rewarded by

WALK 24

128

a magnificent view. You now turn across a plateau called Lilley Hoo, the site of an eighteenth-century racecourse frequented by King George IV, then continue by way of Lilley to Butterfield Green and the fine chalk downs and viewpoints of Warden Hill and Galley Hill near the edge of Luton before returning along the Icknield Way to Treasures Grove.

Starting from the rear end of Treasures Grove Picnic Area, go through a gap by a motorcycle trap and follow the wide grassy Icknield Way (HX10/LL24) straight on towards Telegraph Hill. After a quarter mile the Way becomes tree-lined, then, after a further quarter mile at a fork, keep right. If wishing to see the extensive view of lowland Bedfordshire from the hilltop, go straight on up the hill. Otherwise, fork immediately right again onto bridleway LL9, a grassy track uphill into a copse. At the far side of the copse, continue to follow a winding grassy track uphill to reach a tumulus to your right. Here bear half left across a large field at the northern end of Lilley Hoo, passing the corner of a hedge by a V-shaped oak tree, then bearing slightly left towards a hedge gap into a wood where the trunk of an oak tree is clearly visible. Halfway across this part of the field, turn half right onto a crossing bridleway (still on LL9), heading for the near left-hand corner of a distant wood. By the corner of a hedge, ignore a branching bridleway to your left and keep straight on to reach the near left-hand corner of the wood. Now follow its outside edge straight on to the far end of the wood where you bear slightly left across the field, passing right of a wooden pylon to reach the corner of a hedge. Here bear slightly right and follow a left-hand hedge to enter a green lane called Lilleyhoo Land. Take this lane straight on downhill with views towards Great Offley ahead to reach a bend in a macadam road near Lilley Hoo Farm.

Take this road straight on for 30 yards then, joining the Chiltern Way, turn right through a hedge gap onto path LL4. Now follow a right-hand hedge straight on for nearly half a mile over the top of a hill with wide views of Lilley Bottom ahead and to your left. At the far end of the field, cross a stile and bear half right across the next field, heading just right of some barns at Church Farm to a stile. Cross this and go straight across a field heading left of Lilley Church to reach the near left-hand corner of a fenced orchard, then follow the orchard fence straight on to a kissing-gate. Here continue between hedges to Lilley village street near the church, where you turn left.

Lilley Church was almost completely rebuilt in 1871 by Thomas Jekyll, but retains the chancel arch of its twelfth-century predecessor together with some lavish monuments to members of the Docwra family.

After some 50 yards, turn right onto path LL2 into the car park of the Cassell Memorial Hall, following its right-hand hedge into a green lane. Where this lane turns right, leave it and go straight on into a field following its right-hand hedge (later on path LL3) past Lilleypark Wood. At the far end of the field, go straight on through a gap in the county boundary hedge and take path SL34 straight on uphill, passing just left of a single oak tree near the top and continuing to a hedge gap left of Whitehill Farm. Here cross a stile and bear slightly left towards a distant barn, crossing a field diagonally (soon on path LU26) to cross a stile under an ash tree leading to Butterfield Green Road.

Turn right onto this road and where it forks, go left onto bridleway SL31, a wide farm road with extensive views opening across Luton to your left and towards Warden Hill ahead. After passing Whitehill Wood to your right, at a crossways go straight on for a further quarter mile. At a right-hand bend, fork left onto path SL26, following a sporadic left-hand hedge and later a line of trees, swinging left and descending. At the bottom corner of the field, turn right and on passing through a kissing-gate, turn left onto a path into scrubland on the slopes of Warden Hill keeping the line of trees to your left. After some 300 yards, where the tall trees to your left end, look out for a marker post indicating path SL28 to your right. Turn right onto this and follow its winding course steeply uphill to the top of Warden Hill, where panoramic views open out over Luton and towards the back of the Chiltern escarpment ahead.

Here join a right-hand fence and follow it straight on along the ridge just left of its crest. At the far end of the ridge, go through a kissing-gate, then 100 yards further on, by a marker post, bear half right onto a permissive path descending to a kissing gate onto fenced bridleway SL27 in a dip. Turn right onto this, then, where the left-hand fence ends, turn left rejoining bridleway SL31 and following the left-hand fence gradually swinging left. At a corner of the field, ignore a gate and a stile in the fence and turn right, still following the fence up Galley Hill, the name of which is believed to be a corruption of 'Gallows Hill', as the remains of fifteenth-century gallows victims as well as fourth-century and neolithic corpses have been found in one of the ancient barrows scattered across the hill.

On reaching a gate in front of you, go through it, disregarding a branching path to your right, and continue through patchy scrub over the top of Galley Hill and one of the barrows, then descend gradually to a bridlegate leading onto a golf course. Here look to your right to check that no golfer is driving towards you, then go straight on across a fairway to a gap right of two small silver birches. Now follow a right-hand hedge straight on past a green to a chalky track, onto which you turn left to reach a hedge gap leading to the Icknield Way. Leaving the Chiltern Way, turn right into this ancient green lane (SL23) and follow it (later as SL41, then HX8/LL23) straight on for three-quarters of a mile, joining the reverse direction of Walk 23 at the first crossways, later leaving it again and eventually emerging through a gap by a gate onto a bend in the Hexton road. Now follow this road straight on to your starting point.

WALK 25: Pegsdon (North)

Length of Walk: 8.0 miles / 12.9 Km
Starting Point: Entrance to cul-de-sac road at Pegsdon village green.
Grid Ref: TL119303
Maps: OS Landranger Sheet 166
OS Explorer Sheet 193
OS Pathfinder Sheet 1048 (TL03/13)

How to get there / Parking: Pegsdon, 4 miles west of Hitchin, may be reached from the town by taking the B655 towards Barton-le-Clay and following it for 4 miles, then turning right into a road signposted to Pegsdon and Shillington. After less than 100 yards, turn left into a wide cul-de-sac road where you can park.

Pegsdon, a tiny village with a green and a pub at the foot of the Chiltern escarpment below Deacon Hill, has always been a hamlet of the Bedfordshire parish of Shillington surrounded on three sides by Hertfordshire. In contrast, its mother village of Shillington, which is visited in the course of this walk, with its prominent hilltop church and a wealth of attractive brick cottages gives the impression of having once been a place of some importance.

The walk, by Chiltern standards one of a very easy nature for its length, involving only one climb of any significance, keeps criss-crossing the county boundary, first leading you along the foot of the hills to the Hertfordshire village of Hexton. You then strike out across the lowlands with wide views to reach the Bedfordshire village of Shillington and its vantage point of Church Hill. From here it continues with more wide views to the Hertfordshire village of Pirton with its picturesque cottages and Norman church and castle earthworks before returning over the escarpment outcrop of Knocking Hoe with its superb views of the lowlands to Pegsdon.

Starting from the entrance to the cul-de-sac road on Pegsdon village green, take the Shillington road and follow it for a quarter mile, then turn left into a cul-de-sac road to Bury Farm and some cottages. Just past the farm, where its macadam surface ends, take its rough continuation (bridleway SH4) straight on, soon joining the edge of a tree belt and bearing right. At a signposted junction at the far end of the tree belt, turn left, still following the rough road beside the tree belt. On passing an old watermill known as Hexton Mill, where you enter Hertfordshire, the road called Mill Lane becomes macadamed again. Now follow it for a further half mile, wiggling left at one point, then turning sharp left to reach the edge of Hexton.

At a left-hand bend about 100 yards short of the start of Hexton village, turn sharp right onto path HX6, heading for the right-hand edge of a small area of scrub ahead, with views of Higham Gobion's fourteenth-century church on a hilltop to your left and Shillington Church on a hilltop to your right and later the escarpment behind you. At the far end of the scrub bear slightly right, aiming for a clump of bushes left of a low copse. Here take a grassy track beside a right-hand ditch straight on. Where the track and ditch bear left, go straight on over a footbridge and head for the left-hand end of a hedge ahead. Here cross a footbridge at the county boundary and turn right onto path SH18, following a right-hand hedge and ditch, later a stream, to a field corner. Now turn left onto path SH19 following the right-hand hedge and stream for a further half mile through two fields. On nearing Chalkeybush Farm at Apsley End, the path bears slightly left away from the stream, soon joining a right-hand hedge and following it to cross a stile by a gate to reach a road.

Cross this and take path SH20 straight on between gardens to a kissing-gate. Now follow a left-hand fence straight on through a paddock. At the far end of the paddock, turn left through a kissing-gate and ignoring a second kissing-gate to your left, take path SH42 following a right-hand hedge and stream through two fields. In the second field, by a farm bridge over the stream, take path SH40 bearing half left, following a left-hand fence across a field to a kissing-gate. Now turn right onto enclosed bridleway SH8, soon crossing a bridge to enter a field. Here follow the right-hand hedge straight on, soon with the wall of Shillington churchyard on your left, and climb a series of steps to reach the end of Church Street by the churchyard gate.

Shillington's early fourteenth-century stone church, with its tower rebuilt in brick in 1750 following the collapse of its old tower in 1701, is thought not to have been the first church on this hilltop site and indeed the discovery of ancient coins and Roman pottery on the hill indicates early human habitation. In any event, its elevated location suggests that in mediaeval times the site will have also served a military function as a look-out post.

Now take Church Street straight on. Just past the former village school, turn right onto path SH21, a macadamed alleyway called The Twitchel, and follow it downhill to High Road. Cross this road and a footbridge, then go through a kissing-gate and follow a right-hand fence straight on across a field to a kissing-gate and culvert. Here bear slightly right, heading just right of a gap between low tree belts ahead, with Pirton Church coming into view ahead, to reach a small culvert over a ditch. Cross this and turn right beside the ditch. In a corner of the field, turn left and follow a right-hand hedge. Where the hedge turns right, follow it and later a ditch to a field corner. Here go straight on through a thick hedge at the county boundary, crossing a culvert, then take path PI1 straight on, soon joining a left-hand hedge. Where this hedge turns left, leave it bearing slightly left over the top of a rise, where a fine view opens out towards Pirton ahead and the Chiltern escarpment to your right. When Pirton Church comes into view ahead, aim for it to reach a culvert in a hedge gap. Here bear slightly left, heading for the near end of a hedge ahead with views towards Holwell opening out to your left. By the end of the hedge, cross a culvert and follow a grassy track along the left side of the hedge. Where the hedge ends and the tracks turns right, leave it and turn left across a narrow neck of field to a marker post. Here turn right and follow what is normally a grass crop break to the far end of the field by a clump of trees. Now turn right and follow a sporadic left-hand hedge for 90 yards to a kissing-gate in it. Turn left through this and go straight across the next field to a kissing-gate near a converted timber-framed barn leading to an alleyway. Go through the alleyway, then turn right into West Lane.

Almost immediately turn left by a thatched cottage into a rough lane (still path PI1) which soon narrows to a hedged path and continues past a right-hand field before going through an alleyway to reach the end of a road called Docklands. Go straight on along the road, then, at a T-junction, turn right into Crabtree Lane and almost immediately left onto a hedged macadam path which leads to Toot Hill, then bears left to the churchyard gate.

Toot Hill to your right represents the remains of a Norman motte and bailey castle with an exceptionally large moat built by Ralph de Limesi to command the Hitchin Gap. In the light of its Saxon name 'Toot' meaning 'look-out', it is clear, however, that the Saxons must have previously had a look-out post at this point. The nearby twelfth-century church, like that of Shillington, suffered a collapse of its tower in 1874 and so the present tower dates from its reconstruction in 1876.

By the churchyard gate, turn right onto path PI17, soon passing through a kissing-gate, then follow a right-hand fence across the meadow. Soon after the fence turns right by the corner of the moat,

WALK 25

HOLWELL

135

turn right onto worn path PI18 which leads to a kissing-gate into the end of a village street called Bury End. Follow this road bearing right, then, at a T-junction near the 'Cat and Fiddle', turn left. On reaching Hitchin Road, cross it and take hedged bridleway PI8 known as Wood Lane straight on for nearly a mile. After a third of a mile, the bridleway widens into a green road and starts to climb gently with hedge gaps giving views in places. At the top of the hill known as Knocking Hoe, by Tingley Wood to your left (a Viking name meaning 'meeting-place in a clearing'), where the lane opens out into a field and forks, turn right onto bridleway SH2, recrossing the county boundary and following a right-hand hedge. By the corner of a wood called Tingley Field Plantation, fork right through gates onto path SH16, a winding farm track down the hillside offering superb views across lowland Bedfordshire. To your right, you pass a strange-looking combe with terraces, possibly the result of chalk quarrying, backed by Knocking Hoe which is capped by a Neolithic barrow known as Knocking Knoll due to ghostly knocking sounds said to emanate from it. On reaching a crossing hedge line, turn left onto a grassy track following the right-hand side of the hedge over two rises. At the far end of the field, turn right and follow a sporadic left-hand hedge bounding an old chalk quarry, soon descending between a left-hand fence and a plantation to steps down onto a green road. Cross this and go straight on down some steps in a hedge gap and across a field, then turn left onto a macadam farm road and follow it for a third of a mile to reach the end of Pegsdon village street near its junction with the B655. Turn right along the village street past the 'Live and Let Live', then, at a T-junction, turn left for your starting point.

WALK 26:   Pegsdon (South)

Length of Walk:	(A) 8.5 miles / 13.6 Km
	(B) 2.1 miles / 3.4 Km
	(C) 6.9 miles / 11.1 Km
Starting Points:	(A/B) Entrance to cul-de-sac road at Pegsdon village green.
	(C) Crossroads near 'Green Man', Great Offley.
Grid Refs:	(A/B) TL119303 / (C) TL142271

Maps: OS Landranger Sheet 166
OS Explorer Sheet 193
OS Pathfinder Sheets 1048 (TL03/13) & 1072 (TL02/12)

How to get there / Parking: (A/B) See Walk 25.
                                             (C) See Walk 27.

Pegsdon, described in Walk 25, at the foot of Deacon Hill and Telegraph Hill, with its good road access, pub and two highly scenic paths up the Chiltern escarpment, is an ideal starting point for walkers to climb and explore some of the finest and least spoilt downs in the whole Chiltern range.

Walks A and B indeed use both these paths to climb Telegraph Hill to the Icknield Way with fine views of the downs and the lowlands beneath; while Walks A and C take the Icknield Way past Deacon Hill and explore the quiet hills around Wellbury and Little Offley interspersed with further fine views across the hills and the Hitchin Gap.

Walks A and B start from the entrance to the cul-de-sac road on Pegsdon village green and lead you up the cul-de-sac to a right-hand bend. Here leave this road and go straight on, crossing a narrow strip of verge and the B655, then turn right along its far verge. At a right-hand bend, turn left through a gap between a gate and a motorcycle trap onto bridleway SH3, following a grassy track uphill along the outside edge of a tree belt with fine views of Deacon Hill to your left and later Telegraph Hill ahead. After nearly two-thirds of a mile, having crossed a rise, at a corner of the field fork right off the track through a hedge gap onto fenced bridleway HX3. Now in Hertfordshire follow it beside a belt of scrub, soon with views of Galley

Hill and Warden Hill near Luton to your right. At the far side of the field, go straight on through a hedge gap onto the Ancient British Icknield Way, which at this point divides into several tracks due, no doubt, to the difficulties for horse-drawn vehicles of climbing Telegraph Hill. Cross the tree-lined lower route and go straight on to reach a parallel track. Turn left onto this, briefly joining the route of Walk 24 and ignoring a branching track to your right, take a grassy track up Telegraph Hill with fine views to your left and behind near the top. At the top of the hill, on reaching the corner of a field, take the grassy track straight on along the edge of the field. At the far side of the field, joining **Walk C**, go straight on into a tree-lined green lane (byway OF53/SH61), rejoining the alternative route of the Icknield Way.

After about 70 yards, **Walk B** turns left through a hedge gap onto path SH17. Now read the last paragraph. **Walks A and C** follow this ancient lane along the county boundary straight on for a mile past Deacon Hill (currently open to the public) with the tall dense hedges eventually giving way to lower ones and the trees petering out to give attractive views of the surrounding hills and lowlands to the north. On reaching a gate, go through a gap beside it and turn right onto the B655, following its generally walkable right-hand verge around a right-hand bend.

Now turn right onto bridleway OF34, a wide rough lane. After some 250 yards, by a tall oak tree, turn left through a hedge gap onto path OF45 heading for a smaller tree on the skyline with a view of High Down to your left. Go straight on past this tree to reach a hedge gap at the far side of the field then follow the outside edge of a plantation straight on. On reaching a corner of the plantation, bear half right across the field following a line of tree stumps to a midfield oak tree. Here bear half right downhill, heading for a stile at the corner of a fence at Old Wellbury, descending a flight of steps and crossing a farm road and the stile. Now follow the right-hand fence downhill through a plantation to cross another stile and farm road, then bear half left uphill to the near corner of Sallow Wood. Here bear half left and take a short green lane along the edge of the wood into a field, then follow a grassy track beside a left-hand hedge straight on downhill through a large field with fine views ahead towards Hitchin and Stevenage, eventually climbing again to reach a green lane (bridleway OF32). Turn left into this lane and follow it to the B655.

Turn right onto this road, then, after some 350 yards, turn right again onto bridleway OF31. Take this green lane straight on for three-quarters of a mile, climbing gently to the top of a ridge where views of Minsbury Hill and Offley Hill open out ahead, then continuing to the bottom of the hill. Here at a fork, go right and follow a grassy track beside a left-hand hedge. After over a third of a mile, on nearing a powerline, turn left into a branching green lane (bridleway OF30) and follow it for a quarter mile over a rise with wide views to your left. At another junction of green lanes turn right (still on OF30) and follow this sunken way called Stocking Lane uphill for a quarter mile. On emerging into a field with views towards the lowlands over your right shoulder, follow a grassy track beside a left-hand hedge straight on through two fields to join a macadam drive. Turn right onto this and follow it to School Lane at Birkitt Hill on the edge of Great Offley. Here **Walk A** turns right, while **Walk C** turns left and follows School Lane back into the village.

Walk C starts from the crossroads near the 'Green Man' at Great Offley (described in Walk 27) and takes School Lane for a quarter mile to cross the bridge over the A505. Now **Walks A and C** follow this quiet winding road for half a mile with views to your right towards Hitchin in places. At a fork by Clouds Hill Farm, take the left-hand option, macadamed bridleway OF33, straight on towards Little Offley, with its fine late Tudor brick manor house coming into view ahead. After entering an avenue of lime trees, at a left-hand bend, fork right off the macadam drive, following a left-hand hedge straight on. Having passed a cottage, turn left onto a crossing track (bridleway OF36) into a farmyard.

Now bear slightly right off the track and across the farmyard and take a track between two black buildings ahead. (From here for the next half mile the route follows a permissive path which can be closed at any time. Should this occur, an alternative route via public rights of way is indicated on the plan, but this tends to be difficult to follow.) Follow this track straight on past the back of Little Offley House, then, at a corner of the field, turning right. Where the track forks, take the right-hand option straight on beside a left-hand hedge, later the edge of Muzzleford Wood. At the far end of the wood turn left, still following its outside edge to a field corner, then turn right and follow a left-hand hedge. Where the hedge turns left, take bridleway OF43, still following the hedge to its end. Now go straight on, soon joining a right-hand hedge and continuing beside it to a field corner. Here take bridleway LL19 straight on through a hedge gap and across a field for about 40 yards to a crossing track. Turn right onto this, now on bridleway LL20, following it into and through a copse, then beside a right-hand hedge to the Icknield Way near Telegraph Hill.

Here **Walk C** turns right onto the Icknield Way (byway OF53/ SH61). Now go back five paragraphs. **Walk A** also turns right onto the Icknield Way (byway OF53/SH61), rejoining **Walk B**, then, after about 70 yards, **Walks A and B** turn left through a hedge gap and kissing-gate onto path SH17, re-entering Bedfordshire. Go straight on across a field to the corner of a hedge, then follow this right-hand hedge straight on with views through the hedge of a deep, steep-sided combe. At a corner of the field, go straight on into a belt of scrub, descending with views in places of the combe backed by Deacon Hill. Eventually you re-emerge from the scrub through a kissing-gate and follow its outside edge straight on downhill with wide views. Where the scrubland ends, take a grassy path straight on over a rise, then downhill to a kissing-gate leading to the B655 opposite your starting point.

WALK 27: Great Offley

Length of Walk: 6.8 miles / 11.0 Km

Starting Point: Crossroads near 'Green Man', Great Offley.

Grid Ref: TL142271

Maps: OS Landranger Sheet 166
OS Explorer Sheet 193
OS Pathfinder Sheet 1072 (TL02/12)

How to get there / Parking: Great Offley, 3 miles southwest
of Hitchin, may be reached from the town by taking the
A505 towards Luton for 2 miles, then forking left onto a
road signposted to Great Offley, Lilley and Kings Walden.
At the village crossroads, turn left into the High Street
and find a suitable parking space, but do **not** use the pub
car park without the landlord's permission.

Great Offley, on the old Hitchin–Luton road at the top of the
Chiltern escarpment, was formerly an important stopping
point for travellers whose horses or legs were weary from the
steep climb. Even today, although the A505 now bypasses the
village, it is still characterised by its old coaching inns. Its
location also makes it an ideal centre for walking as not only
does Great Offley give access to the escarpment with its steep
slopes and spectacular views (explored by Walks 26 and 28),
but, in addition, it offers walks in the quiet and beautiful
Chiltern uplands around Lilley Bottom and Kings Walden. It is
therefore hardly surprising that two leading twentieth-
century walkers, Don Gresswell MBE, for more than 50 years
active in walking and path protection groups and founder of
the Chiltern Society's Rights of Way Group, and Ron Pigram,
well-known author of London Transport and other walks
books, chose to live here. The village also has a long history
being named after King Offa II of Mercia, who is believed to
have had a palace here and died here in 796. In the eighteenth
century it was home to Sir Thomas Salusbury, Judge of the
High Court of Admiralty, who rebuilt his home of Offley Place
and the chancel of the parish church (see Walk 28) where
monuments to himself and other family members are housed.
His niece, Hester Thrale, who often stayed at Offley Place as a
child, also came to prominence as a friend of Dr Johnson.

The walk explores the quiet upland countryside to the south of Great Offley, crossing Lilley Bottom to the hilltop hamlets of Mangrove Green, Cockernhoe and Tea Green before returning by a parallel route and abounds with extensive views of the surrounding hills.

Starting from the crossroads near the 'Green Man', take the Lilley road, soon passing the 'Shaker Brown'. At a right-hand bend, fork left onto a side-road, ignoring Salusbury Lane to your left and taking a narrow road called Luton White Hill straight on out of the village. After a quarter mile just before a cottage where the right-hand hedge ends permitting a fine view ahead towards Lilley, turn left through a gap by a padlocked gate onto path OF11, a grassy track left of the cottage, and follow it beside a left-hand hedge through two fields with wide views across Lilley Bottom to your right. Near the far end of the second field, ignore a branching track to your left and take path OF13 straight on beside a left-hand hedge. Soon, where the hedge and track bear right, continue to follow them past Westbury Wood through two fields and a belt of trees. Where the track turns left, leave it and go straight on, heading for an isolated house in Lilley Bottom to reach a hedge gap by a wooden pylon. Go through this gap and continue straight on to reach a road in front of the house.

Turn left onto this road, then, at the corner of the garden hedge, turn right onto path OF44 following a rough track straight on climbing gently for over three-quarters of a mile until you reach a T-junction of tracks near Mangrove Hall. Here turn right through a former gateway and follow a left-hand fence to a field corner. Turn left here onto path OF50, joining the Chiltern Way and following a left-hand hedge bearing left to reach a gate and kissing-gate. Go through the kissing-gate and take a fenced track then a macadam drive straight on past Mangrove Hall to reach the end of a public road by the 'King William IV' at Mangrove Green.

The twin hilltop hamlets of Mangrove Green and Cockernhoe with their greens and scattered cottages give a deceptively rural impression which belies the fact that both are now less than half a mile from the edge of Luton with its voracious appetite for building land. It is largely the existence of the county boundary which they have to thank for so far being spared the fate of nearby Stopsley which has long been swamped by urban development.

Take the road straight on across the green, then, after it becomes enclosed, at a right-hand bend, leaving the Chiltern Way, fork left onto fenced path OF25, which leads you between a hedge and a fence to a stile into a field. Bear slightly right across the field to cross another stile. Now follow a left-hand hedge straight on to a stile into a fenced path which leads you out to a road at Cockernhoe Green. Turn left onto this road, then at a junction, turn right into Brick Kiln Lane. Follow this winding road for a quarter mile, then, on entering Brickkiln Wood, turn right over a stile by a gate onto path OF3 and immediately forking left and following an obvious path flanked by hazel bushes through the wood. When you emerge from the wood, follow its outside edge, then a left-hand hedge straight on with Luton Airport and the outskirts of the town coming into view to your right. Where the hedge ends, bear slightly right across the field to the corner of a sporadic hedge, then bear half left and follow the hedge to the corner of a garden hedge at Crouchmoor Farm. Here follow this hedge straight on to a gate leading to a road junction, then turn left onto the road into Tea Green.

On reaching the green, keep right at a fork passing the 'White Horse' and continuing out of the hamlet. After a quarter mile, soon after the beginning of a left-hand hedge, turn left through a hedge gap onto path OF23 following what is usually a crop break uphill, soon turning right, then, where the crop break ends, bearing half left across the field to reach the edge of Stubbocks Wood. Here turn right and follow its outside edge with fine views of Lilley Bottom, later passing through a hedge gap and descending into the valley. At the bottom corner of the wood, leave it and go straight on heading for the near right-hand corner of Furzen Wood to reach a hedge gap leading to a road.

Cross the road and take path KW38 straight on through a hedge gap, following the outside edge of Furzen Wood uphill. At a corner of the field, bear slightly left to enter the wood and take a waymarked track straight on through it to emerge into a green lane. Turn left into this lane, ignoring a branching track to your right and later emerging into a field. At the far end of the wood, take a grassy track turning right and climbing to reach a hedge at the top of the field. Here, where the track turns left, leave it and go straight on through a hedge gap, then bear half left across the corner of a field to the near corner of Judkin's Wood. Now bear half right onto a grassy track along the outside edge of the wood at first, then entering a green lane. On re-emerging into the field, by a corner of the wood, turn left onto path KW39 still following its outside edge. Where the edge of the wood turns left again, leave it and bear slightly right across a field to a hedge gap by the corner of a wood called Woodfern Wick. Here ignore a crossing track, go straight on through a gap and follow the outside edge of the wood, then, at a corner of the wood, bear half right across a field to a corner of Angel's Wood. Now take path OF24 along its outside edge to pass through a hedge gap, then bear half right onto path OF12 crossing a field diagonally, heading just left of a group of

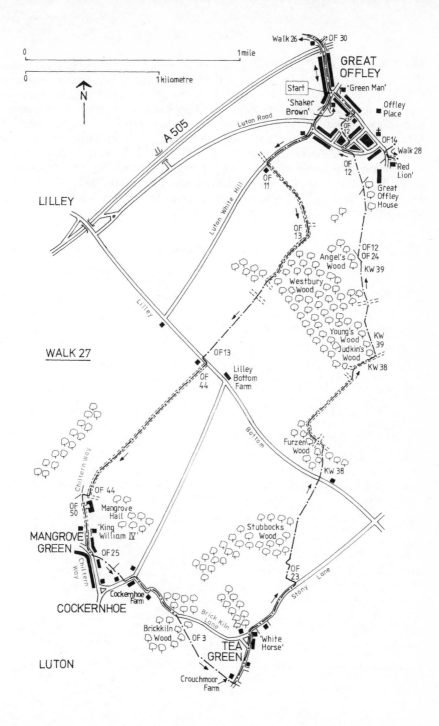

Walk 26

OF 30

GREAT OFFLEY

Start

'Green Man'

'Shaker Brown'

Offley Place

OF 12

OF 14

Walk 28

OF 12

'Red Lion'

Great Offley House

LILLEY

A 505

Luton Road

Luton White Hill

OF 11

OF 13

OF 12
OF 24
KW 39

Angel's Wood

Westbury Wood

Young's Wood

KW 39

Judkin's Wood

KW 38

WALK 27

Lilley

OF 13

OF 44

Lilley Bottom Farm

Bottom

Furzen Wood

KW 38

Chiltern way

OF 44

OF 50

Mangrove Hall

'King William IV'

Stubbocks Wood

MANGROVE GREEN

OF 25

Chiltern Way

OF 23

Stony Lane

COCKERNHOE

Cockernhoe Farm

Brick Kiln Lane

Brickkiln Wood

OF 3

'White Horse'

TEA GREEN

LUTON

Crouchmoor Farm

0 ——— 1mile

0 ——— 1kilometre

N

145

buildings around Great Offley House to reach a concealed stile some 25 yards left of a gate in the far corner of the field. Cross this and follow the outside edge of a copse straight on to a kissing-gate, then go straight on across the next field, heading towards a radio mast behind bungalows ahead, to reach a stile into Salusbury Lane on the edge of Great Offley. Turn left onto this road, then, at a junction, turn right into Gosling Avenue. Just past No. 48, turn left onto path OF12, a fenced concrete drive narrowing by garages, continuing past the end of a cul-de-sac road and crossing the village allotments. Where the path forks, bear right along a stony access road to reach High Street, then turn left for your starting point.

WALK 28:   Hitchin

Length of Walk: 7.4 miles / 11.9 Km

Starting Point: Entrance to car park in Old Charlton Road, Hitchin.

Grid Ref: TL182289

Maps: OS Landranger Sheet 166
OS Explorer Sheet 193
OS Pathfinder Sheet 1072 (TL02/12)

How to get there / Parking: From the Hitchin Hill roundabout at the junction of the A602 and B656, take the B656 towards the town centre. At the next mini-roundabout, turn left into Bridge Street, then after about 300 yards, turn left again into Old Charlton Road, where there is a long-stay car park on your left.

Hitchin, on the River Hiz, a tributary of the Ivel and Great Ouse, at the north-eastern extremity of the Chilterns, is probably the most beautiful town in the whole Chiltern area. Already settled in the Bronze Age, Hitchin and its river only derived their names in the Anglo-Saxon period when the town became the home of the Hicce tribe. It was, however, in the Middle Ages that the town became rich as a centre of the wool trade which supplied the Flanders weavers. This can be seen in St. Mary's Church, a thirteenth-century building lavishly remodelled by rich wool merchants in the fifteenth century. Amongst its many treasures, this massive church contains numerous brasses and a fifteenth-century font with a beautiful carved spire-shaped canopy. Apart from its church, the town, the centre of which retains its mediaeval street pattern, can boast a wealth of picturesque buildings including half-timbered houses with overhangs dating back to the fifteenth and sixteenth centuries and therefore is well worth exploring before or after your walk.

The walk soon leaves the town behind and leads you southwestwards past the hamlets of Charlton, birthplace in 1813 of Sir Henry Bessemer, inventor of an improved steel-making process, and Wellhead at the source of the River Hiz and across the Chiltern foothills with wide views of the escarpment before climbing the escarpment to Great Offley.

WALK 28

148

You then turn southeastwards across the hilltop plateau to near Austage End before descending into a peaceful combe near Offleyholes Farm, crossing further foothills with extensive views and returning into Hitchin.

Starting from the entrance to the car park in Old Charlton Road, Hitchin, turn left onto this road and follow it to its end. Here turn right between anti-cycle barriers onto path H119, passing through an underpass, then turning left onto a macadam path which leads you to the junction of the A602 and Charlton Road. Now turn right into Charlton Road, soon crossing to its left-hand pavement. After some 200 yards at the second road junction, turn left (still on Charlton Road). At a slight left-hand bend, turn right through a white gate, then immediately left onto path H32 heading for the right-hand end of a group of trees right of a cottage, to cross a rail stile by a wooden shed. Now follow a left-hand fence straight on. Where the fence turns left, leave it and go straight on across a field to a hedge gap right of a group of cottages where a stile leads you out to a road at Charlton.

Do not join this road, but instead turn right onto bridleway H33, a rough sunken lane called Windmill Lane, and follow this gently uphill, soon with wide views of the hills to your left. Just past a cottage, where the road ends, go straight on through a gap by a gate into a wide green lane and follow it for a third of a mile. Where the lane opens into a field, follow the right-hand hedge straight on to its end then go straight on across a field to a hedge gap by a storm-damaged beech tree.

Here cross an old green lane called Hoars Lane and take bridleway OF14 straight on through the hedge gap and beside a left-hand hedge for nearly half a mile. On reaching a bend in a green lane by a wooden electricity pylon, turn left into it. After nearly a quarter mile where the lane turns left, leave it, turning right onto path OF14 and following a left-hand hedge. Where the hedge turns left, continue to follow it, eventually passing through a hedge gap by the corner of a wood called Minsbury Plantation. Now follow the outside edge of the wood straight on. At the far side of the wood, turn right through a hedge gap and bear half left across the corner of a field to the corner of a fenced plantation. Now follow the plantation fence, later the outside edge of a mature wood, straight on uphill. At the top corner of the field, there is a fine view behind you across Hitchin and the lowlands to the north. Having admired this view, bear left onto a track into the wood. On leaving the wood, follow its outside edge straight on with views across the hills to your left. At the far end of the field, go straight on through a hedge gap and take a fenced path along the edge of the wood and past the churchyard to a stile onto Great Offley village street near the church and the 'Red Lion'.

The church to your right dates from the thirteenth century, but its chancel was rebuilt in about 1750 by Sir Thomas Salusbury of nearby Offley Place, a judge of the High Court of Admiralty, to display his family monuments, while the tower was rebuilt in brick in 1814. Inside are a beautiful fourteenth-century font and eighteenth-century monuments by Sir Robert Taylor and Nollekens.

Turn left onto this road, then by the 'Red Lion', fork left into a rough lane called Harris Lane. After some 350 yards at a sharp left-hand bend, leave the lane and take bridleway OF22 straight on following a grassy track beside a right-hand hedge. At the far side of the field at two track junctions, go straight on, taking a rough track across a large field to pass through gates at the corner of a wood called Cockrood Spring. Now bear half right, crossing a field diagonally to gates in the right-hand hedge. Go through these and turn left, joining a track beside a left-hand hedge and following it, later the outside edge of West Wood (now on KW36).

At the far end of the field ignore a branching track into the wood and go straight on through a hedge gap. Now take the track straight on through two more fields. At the far end of the second field, where you briefly meet the route of Walk 29, turn left through a hedge gap onto path KW27, following a right-hand hedge to the far side of the field. Here turn right through a hedge gap then immediately left through a second and cross a track by a left-hand gate. Now take path PR7 (later joining bridleway PR6) following the outside edge of West Wood straight on, eventually starting to descend the escarpment. On nearing the bottom corner of the field, the bridleway bears left and drops through a corner of the wood to reach a gate in the valley bottom. Go through this and follow a right-hand hedge straight on along the valley bottom to a gate into a copse. Take the obvious path straight on through the copse to a bridlegate, then follow a right-hand iron parkland fence straight on. Where the iron railings end, go straight on across the field to a gate leading to a bend in a road.

Take this road straight on for nearly a quarter mile passing a copse to your left. At a left-hand bend by the corner of a wood on a hillside to your right, turn right onto bridleway PR8 taking a track uphill to the corner of the wood. Here go straight on along the edge of the wood, through an outcrop of woodland, then beside a right-hand fence. Where the track drops down into the left-hand field, follow it, bearing half left to the corner of a hedge then taking bridleway PR8/IP1 beside a right-hand hedge over the brow of a hill with wide views to your left at first. After nearly half a mile at a corner of the field, go straight on through a hedge gap into an ancient sunken lane called Tatmorehills Lane and turn left into it, soon reaching Maydencroft Lane.

Cross this road and take bridleway H41 straight on through a hedge gap, following a right-hand hedge, which bears left at one point, to reach a hedge gap at the far end of the field. Go through this and turn left to reach Brick Kiln Lane, then cross this road and go through a fence gap opposite into Priory Park. Now bear half right onto path H40 heading between Hitchin Priory, a Palladian eighteenth-century mansion incorporating parts of a fourteenth-century Carmelite priory, and a clump of trees, to reach a signpost by the fence of the A602. Here turn right onto path H120 following the A602 fence to a fence gap leading to a footbridge. Turn left over this footbridge, then at its far end, turn left through a gap in the railings onto path H43 following a left-hand fence through a copse. On reaching a kissing-gate, turn left onto fenced path H38, soon meeting and following the A602 fence (now on path H119). Where the path widens out, follow the right-hand fence, soon passing through a plantation to join the A602 at the River Hiz bridge. Cross this bridge, then fork right onto fenced path H119 which soon leads you to the end of Old Charlton Road where your starting point is straight ahead.

WALK 29: Preston

Length of Walk: 7.3 miles / 11.7 Km

Starting Point: 'Red Lion', Preston.

Grid Ref: TL180247

Maps: OS Landranger Sheet 166
OS Explorer Sheet 193
OS Pathfinder Sheet 1072 (TL02/12)

How to get there / Parking: Preston, some 2.5 miles south of Hitchin, may be reached from the Hitchin Hill roundabout at the junction of the A602 and B656 by taking the road signposted to Gosmore for 2.4 miles, passing through Gosmore and continuing straight on to Preston. At the village green, find a suitable parking space in the side roads around it, but do **not** use the pub car park without the landlord's permission.

Notes: Heavy nettle growth may be encountered in summer, particularly on paths KW49 and KW34.

Preston, with its leafy green, with an attractive well and pub, is the epitome of the English village. Like most villages, it has a long history, its manor of 'Deneslai' being listed in the Domesday Book. In 1147 the manor was given to the Knights Templar, an order of warrior-monks, who held it till their suppression in 1312, and thus it became known as Temple Dinsley. The manor was subsequently held by another monastic order called the Knights Hospitaller before it fell to the Crown in the reformation. The present house, built in 1714 and greatly enlarged by Sir Edwin Lutyens in 1908, is now a private girls' school. The vicinity of Preston, however, also has other religious associations, as nearby Wain Wood was the scene of secret midnight services with massive congregations held by the Puritan writer and preacher John Bunyan, author of 'Pilgrim's Progress', while modern Castle Farm stands on the site of Hunsdon House whose non-conformist occupants also suffered seventeenth-century religious persecution. This same house was converted in the 1760s to resemble a castle (hence the name of the farm) by Captain Robert Hinde, an eccentric retired army officer, whom the contemporary author, Laurence Sterne took as the model for his Uncle Toby in his 'Tristram Shandy'.

The walk leads you from Preston through the quiet, rolling hill country around King's Walden to the west, crossing Lilley Bottom to the hilltop village of Breachwood Green, before returning by a parallel route.

Starting from the 'Red Lion' at Preston, take the Hitchin road. After about 120 yards, fork left into Chequers Lane. On passing a row of cottages called Chequers Cottages, turn left through a small gate onto path PR4 passing between hedges to enter a recreation ground. Now follow its right-hand hedge straight on. At the far side of the recreation ground, go through a hedge gap and continue between a hedge and a line of fence posts to reach Butcher's Lane. Turn left onto this road and after about 35 yards, turn right through a concealed kissing-gate onto path PR5. Now bear slightly right across a field, passing right of a black wooden cowshed to reach two large holly bushes. Here bear half left following a sporadic line of trees to a gate, then bear slightly right, following the right-hand hedge to a kissing-gate leading into Dead Woman's Lane (KW48), part of an ancient road from Hitchin to Kimpton.

Turn right into this green lane and follow it for some 300 yards. Where its left-hand hedge ends, turn left, ignoring a track to your left, and take path KW37 across a field heading just right of a black barn with a red-tiled roof at Austage End, to reach a sunken green lane by two holly trees. Turn left into this lane (KW46) and after about 120 yards, by a marker post just beyond the first right-hand oak tree, turn right onto path KW 37 crossing a field to the left-hand end of a line of oaks. Here bear slightly left and follow a right-hand hedge to a corner of the field, then bear slightly right and take a narrow fenced path beside a left-hand hedge passing left of a large new house to reach a road at Austage End.

Turn left onto this road and after about 50 yards at a left-hand bend, turn right onto a grassy track (KW36), passing through a hedge gap and bearing right to follow a right-hand hedge. At the far side of the field, follow the track wiggling to the right through a hedge gap to meet the route of Walk 28, then turn left onto path KW27 following a left-hand hedge. Where the hedge turns right, go straight on through a hedge gap and across the corner of a field to a hedge gap by the left-hand of two oak trees. Now go straight on across the next field to a hedge gap leading into a green lane. Turn right into this lane, immediately bearing left and descending to reach Stopsley Holes Farm.

Here take a track straight on between the farm buildings to the end of a road. Now follow this road straight on uphill for some 300 yards ignoring a branching road to the left. Just after a right-hand bend shaded by overhanging trees, turn left onto path KW25, a grassy track leading up into a field. On reaching the edge of the field, turn sharp right, passing through a bridlegate onto path KW49. Now follow this hedged path straight on for some 250 yards, crossing two stiles and eventually reaching a road. Turn left onto this road and after some 60 yards, before reaching a powerline, turn right through a hedge gap onto path KW12 bearing slightly left across a field, with wide views of Lilley Bottom opening out ahead, to reach the corner of a hedge at the left-hand end of a line of oaks. Now bear half right across the next field to the corner of a hedge. Here go through a hedge gap and follow a right-hand hedge downhill. At the bottom end of the field, follow the hedge turning right, then, at a corner, go straight on through the hedge into the next field. Now turn left and follow the left-hand hedge downhill to the road in Lilley Bottom.

Cross this road bearing slightly left and take path KW33 following a left-hand hedge gently uphill. After some 200 yards, where the hedge turns left, follow it to a corner of the field, then turn right and follow the winding left-hand hedge, later a crop break. Where the crop break widens into an area of scrub, keep left of the scrub and follow its outside edge uphill with fine views of Lilley Bottom to your left and Darleyhall Windmill soon coming into view ahead. At the top corner of the field, go straight on into a green lane and follow it to the end of a road at The Heath, a hamlet on the edge of Breachwood Green.

Continue along this road, ignoring a branching road to the right, then, at a T-junction, take the major road straight on over a crossroads towards Breachwood Green, another village connected with John Bunyan as the pulpit he used when preaching at nearby Bendish in 1658 is housed in the village's hundred-year-old Baptist chapel. After the right-hand houses end, at a right-hand bend, turn left through a hedge gap onto path KW14, following this obvious path to the end of a hedge. Here bear slightly right and later bear slightly left to enter Lord's Wood. Follow the obvious path straight on through the wood, then at its far side, ignore a branching path to the right and follow the outside edge of the wood, later a left-hand hedge, straight on downhill to the road in Lilley Bottom.

Cross this road and a stile opposite, then bear slightly right uphill to cross a stile in a clump of trees right of the top corner of the field leading into Garden Wood. In the wood turn left onto path KW19 which soon emerges over a stile into a field. Here turn right and follow the outside edge of the wood, then where it turns right by a tall oak, leave it and go straight on downhill and up again with glimpses of Kingswalden Bury, rebuilt in neo-Georgian style in 1972 to replace a Victorian predecessor, through the trees to your right, to reach a gate onto King's Walden village street.

WALK 29

155

The name King's Walden is derived from the village having been a royal manor in a wooded area. Its thirteenth-century church with its notable fourteenth-century painted screen and a tower from the same period contains memorials to the Hale family who lived at the Bury from 1595 to 1885.

Turn right onto the village street and follow it for nearly 300 yards passing the church and a large red-brick house, then near a black cowshed, turn right through gates onto path KW23, passing through two further gateways, then crossing a parkland field with a clear view of Kingswalden Bury to your right at one point, heading somewhat left of a tall cedar and an electricity pole to reach a kissing-gate onto a tree-lined drive. Go through this and another kissing-gate opposite, then bear slightly right along a worn path which joins a slightly raised grass causeway. After 140 yards, by a large oak tree to your left and a marker post, bear half left onto path KW34 across the parkland passing right of two clumps of trees to reach a kissing-gate onto a road opposite Whitehall House.

Turn right onto this road, soon ignoring a branching road to the left, then at a second road junction, turn left onto the Preston and Hitchin road. After some 70 yards, just past a right-hand barn, turn right through a gap by metal gates onto path KW30 into the farmyard. At the rear of the farmyard, bear half left across the field, heading for a point 60 yards right of the far right-hand corner of a wood to your left, eventually descending a steep bank to join a road. Cross this and take path PR12 through a hedge gap virtually opposite, descending a steep bank, then bearing half left across the field to its far left-hand corner. Here go through the left-hand of two hedge gaps and bear right following the right-hand hedge through four fields to a gate and kissing-gate leading to a road on the outskirts of Preston. Turn left onto this road, then at a fork go left. Just past Preston Primary School on the right, turn right onto enclosed macadam path PR3 and follow this through to a cul-de-sac lane which leads you out to the village green near the 'Red Lion'.

Length of Walk: (A)   7.2 miles / 11.5 Km
                            (B)   2.5 miles / 4.0 Km
                            (C)   5.2 miles / 8.3 Km

Starting Point: Southern entrance gates to St. Paul's Walden churchyard.

Grid Ref: TL193222

Maps: OS Landranger Sheet 166
          OS Explorer Sheet 193
          OS Pathfinder Sheet 1072 (TL02/12)

How to get there / Parking: St. Paul's Walden, some 4.3 miles south of Hitchin, may be reached from the town by taking the B656 towards Codicote for about 2.5 miles, then turning right onto the B651 towards Whitwell. After some 1.8 miles, at a crossroads by the 'Strathmore Arms', turn right onto a road signposted to St. Paul's Walden Church and park by the church avoiding blocking field entrances. In case of difficulty, Walks A and B can also be started from Whitwell, where on-street parking is possible in places.

Notes: Heavy nettle growth may be encountered in summer on Walks A and C, particularly on path PW12 and bridleway LA17.

St. Paul's Walden, set in hillside parkland above the Mimram valley in the far north-east corner of the Chilterns, is probably best known as the birthplace in 1900 of Queen Elizabeth the Queen Mother, daughter of the Earl of Strathmore, whose family, the Bowes-Lyons (formerly Bowes), have owned St. Paul's Waldenbury for more than 200 years. The present house, which can be seen from Walks A and B, was built in 1767 and considerably extended in 1887. The parish church, where the Queen Mother was christened and which she attended as a child, dates from the fourteenth century and has a chancel rebuilt by Edward Gilbert in 1727. When this church was built, however, the village had another name as it was then called Abbot's Walden because the manor belonged to

0 _____ 1mile

0 _____ 1kilometre

CHAPELFOOT

LA1

B 656

'Royal Oak'

LA2

A/C

B 651

Poynders End Farm

PRESTON

Reservoir

PR 2

LA1

B 656

Minsden Chapel

Minsden Chapel Plantation

Lady Grove

LA 2

Hill End Farm

LA17

LANGLEY END

LA 16

Hitch Wood

LA19/PR16

PW 35

Pinfold Wood

Foxholes Wood

LA 3

B651

N

PW12
PW9

Stagenhoe Home Farm

Lodges

Hitch Spring

Stagenhoe Garden Wood

A/C

PW 9

PW 7

A/B

PW8

C

A/C

B

ST. PAUL'S WALDEN

Walk Wood

Start

PW 3

'Strathmore Arms'

A/B

St. Paul's Waldenbury

PW8

PW 3

PW 2

B 651

WALK 30

River 'Bull'

Mimram

WHITWELL

B 651

'Maidens Head'

158

St. Alban's Abbey, but during the reformation, the manor passed to St. Paul's Cathedral and so was renamed St. Paul's Walden in 1544. The royal wedding in 1923 did not, however, create the village's first royal connection, as there is a memorial in the church to Henry Stapleford who died in 1631, having acted as servant to three very different monarchs, Elizabeth I, James I and Charles I.

Walks A and B lead you southwards from the village through attractive parkland with fine views, to the olde worlde village of Whitwell in the picturesque Mimram valley, while Walks A and C explore the wooded hills to the north dropping to Chapelfoot in the Ippollitts valley before returning by way of the ruins of Minsden Chapel and the hamlet of Langley End to St. Paul's Walden.

Starting from the southern entrance gates to St. Paul's Walden churchyard, **Walk C** turns right along the road and follows it straight on for a quarter mile to where its macadam surface ends by the site of an old lodge. Now take its stony continuation, path PW9, straight on and omit the next two paragraphs.

Walks A and B also start from these gates, but cross the road and take path PW3, a fenced track, straight on descending gently for a quarter mile through old parkland. By a cottage called 'The Garden House', take a macadam drive straight on, ignoring a branching drive to the left and continuing uphill to cross an avenue of trees where you can obtain a view of St. Paul's Waldenbury to your right. On rounding a right-hand bend, fork left through a kissing-gate by a field gate onto path PW2 and bear half left, following a line of trees across a parkland field to a kissing-gate between gates where a view of Whitwell (pronounced 'Whittle') in the Mimram valley opens out ahead. Now follow a right-hand fence downhill to cross a stile and farm road then continue to a gate and stile leading to a footbridge over the River Mimram (until recent years often given the alternative name of Maran). Cross this bridge and bear slightly left across a field to a gate and stile, then follow a rough drive bearing right to reach the B651, Whitwell High Street, with its ancient inns and cottages.

Turn right onto this road and follow it through the village, then, just past the post office by a half-timbered cottage called The Tannery, turn right into a cul-de-sac road known as The Valley, soon recrossing the Mimram. Where its macadam surface ends, take its stony continuation straight on up a deep tree-lined sunken lane. Where the lane forks, turn left onto path PW8 to reach a gate into a field. Do **not** go through this gate, but turn right through a kissing-gate into another field, then turn left and follow a left-hand hedge. At the far end of the field, turn right and follow a left-hand hedge uphill. At the next corner, turn right again and after a few yards, turn left through a kissing-gate. Now follow the left-hand hedge straight on through two fields to a kissing-gate into Walk Wood. In this wood follow a winding path straight on, soon passing a field to your left. About 150 yards beyond the far side of the field the path turns sharp right, then 100 yards further on, it turns sharp left. Eventually a field comes into view to your left and you soon leave the wood and follow a hedge path to reach the end of a macadam road by the site of an old lodge of Stagenhoe Park where **Walk B** turns right onto the road and follows it straight on back to your starting point, while **Walk A** turns left onto the road's stony continuation (path PW9).

Walks A and C now follow the track's winding course past Garden Wood and an unusual Jacobean cottage to reach the macadam drive to Stagenhoe Park. Mentioned in the Domesday Book, its present house was built in 1737 and is now a Sue Ryder Home. In the 1880s it was occupied by Sir Arthur Sullivan, who composed 'The Mikado' here and outraged local people by his life-style. Turn left onto the drive (still path PW9) with views of the house to your left. Where the drive forks by a white gate, fork right off it and follow a grassy path beside a left-hand fence straight on to a corner of the field. Here go straight on through a hedge gap then turn right through a second hedge gap to reach a barbed-wire fence. Now turn right onto path PW12 into and through Foxholes Wood. On re-emerging into a field, turn left and follow the edge of the wood, then a garden fence to reach a farm road by a cottage.

Turn left onto the farm road passing the cottage. By some outbuildings, turn right onto path PW35 following the outside edge of Pinfold Wood. At a corner of the wood, leave it and bear half right across a field to a hedge gap into Hitch Wood. Here take path LA19/PR16, a wide winding track between mossy banks straddling the parish boundary between Langley and Preston, straight on for over a third of a mile, later with a field visible to your left. On reaching a T-junction with another track, turn right onto it and follow it to the end of a macadam road by some cottages. Now take this road straight on to a T-junction where you turn left soon passing the former Minsden Farm.

At a road junction take the Gosmore and Hitchin road straight on, then after about 70 yards, turn right through a hedge gap onto path PR2, following this narrow fenced path past an underground reservoir to a stile. Now follow a right-hand hedge straight on, turning left at a corner of the field and continuing until you reach a stile in the hedge. Here transfer to the other side of the hedge and take path LA1 still following the hedge to Poynders End Farm with its fine wooden barns and timber-framed farmhouse. Go straight on past the farm, then take a grassy track beside a left-hand hedge. Where the hedge turns left, follow the grassy track straight on with wide views across the valley towards Hitchin to your left and Stevenage beyond the next rise. Eventually the track joins a right-hand hedge which you follow to the B656 at Chapelfoot.

Turn right onto this road and follow it past the 'Royal Oak', part of which dates from the seventeenth century. At the far end of the pub garden, before reaching a black wooden barn, turn right onto bridleway LA2 passing the end of the pub and turning left by a large chestnut tree into a fenced path. On emerging into a field, follow the left-hand hedge straight on gently climbing. Where the hedge ends, keep straight on, heading just left of the ruins of Minsden Chapel to reach the corner of Minsden Chapel Plantation near the chapel ruins.

Built in the fourteenth century, Minsden Chapel was a chapel-of -ease of Hitchin parish serving the lost hamlet of 'Minlesden' referred to in the Domesday Book. By 1650 the hamlet would seem to have disappeared as the chapel was already reported to be in a decayed state and during the last recorded service at the chapel, a marriage in 1738, the curate is believed to have narrowly missed being struck by falling masonry. In the early twentieth century, the noted local historian, Reginald Hine, who was fascinated by these allegedly haunted ruins, leased them from the Church of England and was subsequently buried here in 1949.

Now follow the outside edge of the wood, later a right-hand hedge, straight on downhill. Where the hedge ends, follow the bridleway bearing slightly left then right across the field to a hedge gap leading to the B651. Turn right onto this road, then fork immediately left onto bridleway LA17 which climbs gently through hillside scrubland. On reaching a grassy track, turn left onto it to reach the end of a macadam road by Hill End Farm at Langley End. Take this road straight on, then at a left-hand bend, fork right onto path LA16 passing through a copse to cross a stile. Now take a track beside a right-hand hedge straight on, ignoring a branching track to the right. At the far end of the field, bear right between hedges to cross a stile into a hedged path. Follow its winding course to a narrow road, then turn left onto the road and immediately right over a stile onto path LA3 heading for the right-hand end of a coniferous plantation to cross a stile. Now go straight on, at first skirting the conifers, then continuing ahead to join a track straight on through a copse called Hitch Spring to reach the B651.

Turn left onto this road passing the lodge gates of Stagenhoe Park surmounted by a stag and wrought-ironwork, then on rounding a left-hand bend, turn right through a hedge gap onto path PW7, bearing left across a field following a line of three trees to reach the corner of a hedge. Here follow the left-hand hedge straight on and on nearing a cottage, bear slightly left onto a path between a hedge and a fence leading to a narrow road at St. Paul's Walden. Turn left onto this road passing the White House, then at a left-hand bend, fork right onto path PW3 passing through the churchyard to reach your starting point.

Index of Place Names

Books Published by THE BOOK CASTLE

CHANGES IN OUR LANDSCAPE: Aspects of Bedfordshire, Buckinghamshire and the Chilterns 1947-1992: Eric Meadows. Over 350 photographs from the author's collection spanning nearly 50 years.

COUNTRYSIDE CYCLING IN BEDFORDSHIRE, BUCKINGHAMSHIRE AND HERTFORDSHIRE: Mick Payne. Twenty rides on and off-road for all the family.

PUB WALKS FROM COUNTRY STATIONS: Bedfordshire and Hertfordshire: Clive Higgs. Fourteen circular country rambles, each starting and finishing at a railway station and incorporating a pub stop at a mid way point.

PUB WALKS FROM COUNTRY STATIONS: Buckinghamshire and Oxfordshire: Clive Higgs. Circular rambles incorporating pub-stops.

LOCAL WALKS: South Bedfordshire and North Chilterns: Vaughan Basham. Twenty-seven thematic circular walks.

LOCAL WALKS: North and Mid Bedfordshire: Vaughan Basham. Twenty-five thematic circular walks.

FAMILY WALKS: Chilterns South: Nick Moon. Thirty 3 to 5 mile circular walks.

FAMILY WALKS: Chilterns North: Nick Moon. Thirty shorter circular walks.

CHILTERN WALKS: Hertfordshire, Bedfordshire and North Bucks: Nick Moon.

CHILTERN WALKS: Buckinghamshire: Nick Moon.

CHILTERN WALKS: Oxfordshire and West Buckinghamshire: Nick Moon. A trilogy of circular walks, in association with the Chiltern Society. Each volume contains 30 circular walks.

OXFORDSHIRE WALKS: Oxford, the Cotswolds and the Cherwell Valley: Nick Moon.

OXFORDSHIRE WALKS: Oxford, the Downs and the Thames Valley: Nick Moon. Two volumes that complement Chiltern Walks: Oxfordshire, and complete coverage of the county, in association with the Oxford Fieldpaths Society. Thirty circular walks in each.

THE D'ARCY DALTON WAY: Nick Moon. Long-distance footpath across the Oxfordshire Cotswolds and Thames Valley, with various circular walk suggestions.

THE CHILTERN WAY: Nick Moon. A guide to the new 133 mile circular Long-Distance Path through Bedfordshire, Buckinghamshire,Hertfordshire and Oxfordshire, as planned by the Chiltern Society.

JOURNEYS INTO BEDFORDSHIRE: Anthony Mackay. Foreword by The Marquess of Tavistock, Woburn Abbey. A lavish book of over 150 evocative ink drawings.

COCKNEY KID & COUNTRYMEN: Ted Enever. The Second World War remembered by the children of Woburn Sands and Aspley Guise. A six year old boy is evacuated from London's East End to start life in a Buckinghamshire village.

BUCKINGHAM AT WAR: Pip Brimson. Stories of courage, humour and pathos as Buckingham people adapt to war.

WINGS OVER WING: The Story of World War II Bomber Training Unit: Mike Warth. The activities of RAF Wing in Buckinghamshire.

JOURNEYS INTO BUCKINGHAMSHIRE: Anthony Mackay. Superb line drawings plus background text: large format landscape gift book.

BUCKINGHAMSHIRE MURDERS: Len Woodley. Nearly two centuries of nasty crimes.

WINGRAVE: A Rothschild Village in the Vale: Margaret and Ken Morley. Thoroughly researched and copiously illustrated survey of the last 200 years in this lovely village between Aylesbury and Leighton Buzzard.

HISTORIC FIGURES IN THE BUCKINGHAMSHIRE LANDSCAPE: John Houghton. Major personalities and events that have shaped the county's past, including Bletchley Park.

TWICE UPON A TIME: John Houghton. North Bucks short stories loosely based on fact.

SANCTITY AND SCANDAL IN BEDS AND BUCKS: John Houghton. A miscellany of unholy people and events.

MANORS and MAYHEM, PAUPERS and PARSONS: Tales from Four Shires: Beds., Bucks., Herts. and Northants: John Houghton. Little known historical snippets and stories.

THE LAST PATROL: Policemen killed on duty while serving the counties of Berkshire, Buckinghamshire and Oxfordshire: Len Woodley.

FOLK: Characters and Events in the History of Bedfordshire and Northamptonshire: Vivienne Evans. Anthology of people of yesteryear - arranged alphabetically by village or town.

JOHN BUNYAN: His Life and Times: Vivienne Evans. Highly praised and readable account.

THE RAILWAY AGE IN BEDFORDSHIRE: Fred Cockman. Classic, illustrated account of early railway history.

A LASTING IMPRESSION: Michael Dundrow. A boyhood evacuee recalls his years in the Chiltern village of Totternhoe near Dunstable.

GLEANINGS REVISITED: Nostalgic Thoughts of a Bedfordshire Farmer's Boy: E.W. O'Dell. His own sketches and early photographs adorn this lively account of rural Bedfordshire in days gone by.

BEDFORDSHIRE'S YESTERYEARS Vol 2: The Rural Scene: Brenda Fraser-Newstead. Vivid first-hand accounts of country life two or three generations ago.

BEDFORDSHIRE'S YESTERYEARS Vol 3: Craftsmen and Tradespeople: Brenda Fraser-Newstead. Fascinating recollections over several generations practising many vanishing crafts and trades.

BEDFORDSHIRE'S YESTERYEARS Vol 4: War Times and Civil Matters: Brenda Fraser-Newstead. Two World Wars, plus transport, law and order, etc.

DUNNO'S ORIGINALS: A facsimile of the rare pre-Victorian history of Dunstable and surrounding villages. New preface and glossary by John Buckledee, Editor of The Dunstable Gazette.

PROUD HERITAGE: A Brief History of Dunstable, 1000-2000AD: Vivienne Evans. Century by century account of the town's rich tradition and key events, many of national significance.

DUNSTABLE WITH THE PRIORY: 1100-1550: Vivienne Evans. Dramatic growth of Henry I's important new town around a major crossroads.

DUNSTABLE IN TRANSITION: 1550-1700: Vivienne Evans. Wealth of original material as the town evolves without the Priory.

OLD DUNSTABLE: Bill Twaddle. A new edition of this collection of early photographs.

BOURNE and BRED: A Dunstable Boyhood Between the Wars: Colin Bourne. An elegantly written, well illustrated book capturing the spirit of the town over fifty years ago.

OLD HOUGHTON: Pat Lovering. Pictorial record capturing the changing appearances of Houghton Regis over the past 100 years.

ROYAL HOUGHTON: Pat Lovering. Illustrated history of Houghton Regis from the earliest of times to the present.

GIRLS IN BLUE: Christine Turner. The activities of the famous Luton Girls Choir properly documented over its 41 year period from 1936 to 1977.

THE STOPSLEY BOOK: James Dyer. Definitive, detailed account of this historic area of Luton. 150 rare photographs.

THE STOPSLEY PICTURE BOOK: James Dyer. New material and photographs make an ideal companion to The Stopsley Book.

PUBS and PINTS: The Story of Luton's Public Houses and Breweries: Stuart Smith. The background to beer in the town, plus hundreds of photographs, old and new.

LUTON AT WAR - VOLUME ONE: As compiled by The Luton News in 1947, a well illustrated thematic account.

LUTON AT WAR - VOLUME TWO: Second part of the book compiled by The Luton News.

THE CHANGING FACE OF LUTON: An Illustrated History: Stephen Bunker, Robin Holgate and Marian Nichols. Luton's development from earliest times to the present busy industrial town. Illustrated in colour and mono.

WHERE THEY BURNT THE TOWN HALL DOWN: Luton, The First World War and the Peace Day Riots, July 1919: Dave Craddock. Detailed analysis of a notorious incident.

THE MEN WHO WORE STRAW HELMETS: Policing Luton, 1840-1974: Tom Madigan. Fine chronicled history, many rare photographs; author~served in Luton Police for fifty years.

BETWEEN THE HILLS: The Story of Lilley, a Chiltern Village: Roy Pinnock. A priceless piece of our heritage - the rural beauty remains but the customs and way of life described here have largely disappeared.

KENILWORTH SUNSET: A Luton Town Supporter's Journal: Tim Kingston. Frank and funny account of football's ups and downs.

A HATTER GOES MAD!: Kristina Howells. Luton Town footballers, officials and supporters talk to a female fan.

LEGACIES: Tales and Legends of Luton and the North Chilterns: Vic Lea. Mysteries and stories based on fact, including Luton Town Football Club. Many photographs.

THREADS OF TIME: Shela Porter. The life of a remarkable mother and businesswoman, spanning the entire century and based in Hitchin and (mainly)Bedford.

STICKS AND STONES: The Life and Times of a Journeyman Printer in Hertford, Dunstable, Cheltenham and Wolverton: Harry Edwards.

LEAFING THROUGH LITERATURE: Writers' Lives in Herts and Beds: David Carroll. Illustrated short biographies of many famous authors and their connections with these counties.

A PILGRIMAGE IN HERTFORDSHIRE: H.M. Alderman. Classic, between-the-wars tour round the county, embellished with line drawings.

THE VALE OF THE NIGHTINGALE: Molly Andrews. Several generations of a family, lived against a Harpenden backdrop.

SUGAR MICE AND STICKLEBACKS: Childhood Memories of a Hertfordshire Lad: Harry Edwards.Vivid evocation of gentle pre-war in an archetypal village, Hertingfordbury.

SWANS IN MY KITCHEN: Lis Dorer. Story of a Swan Sanctuary near Hemel Hempstead.

THE HILL OF THE MARTYR: An Architectural History of St.Albans Abbey: Eileen Roberts. Scholarly and readable chronological narrative history of Hertfordshire and Bedfordshire's famous cathedral. Fully illustrated with photographs and plans.

THE TALL HITCHIN INSPECTOR'S CASEBOOK: A Victorian Crime Novel Based on Fact: Edgar Newman. Worthies of the time encounter more archetypal villains.

SPECIALLY FOR CHILDREN

VILLA BELOW THE KNOLLS: A Story of Roman Britain: Michael Dundrow. An exciting adventure for young John in Totternhoe and Dunstable two thousand years ago.

THE RAVENS: One Boy Against the Might of Rome: James Dyer. On the Barton Hills and in the south-east of England as the men of the great fort of Ravensburgh (near Hexton) confront the invaders.

THE BOOK CASTLE, 12 Church Street, Dunstable,
Bedfordshire LU5 4RU
Tel: (01582) 605670 Fax (01582) 662431
Email: bc@book-castle.co.uk